BUILDING YOUR MATE'S SELF-ESTEEM

BUILDING YOUR MATE'S SELF-ESTEEM

Dennis & Barbara Rainey

A
JANET
THOMA
BOOK

THOMAS NELSON PUBLISHERS
Nashville

Published in Nashville, Tennessee, by Thomas Nelson, Inc.

Unless indicated otherwise, Scripture quotations are from *The New American Standard Bible*, © The Lockman Foundation 1960, 1962, 1963, 1968, 1971, 1972, 1975, 1977.

Library of Congress Cataloging-in-Publication Data

Rainey, Dennis, 1948–
    Building your mate's self-esteem / Dennis & Barbara Rainey.
        p.   cm.
    Originally published: San Bernardino, CA : Here's Life Publishers, c1986.
    ISBN 0-8407-4459-5
    1. Marriage — Religious aspects — Christianity.
2. Self-esteem — Religious aspects — Christianity. 3. Inter-personal relations — Religious aspects — Christianity.
I. Rainey, Barbara. II. Title.
[BV835.R345   1993]
248.8′4 — dc20   93-16344
                                                              CIP

Printed in the United States of America

5 6 7 8 9 — 98 97 96 95 94

We dedicate this book to the four people who have had a profoundly positive impact upon our self-esteem — our parents:

Bob and Jean Peterson

and

Ward and Dalcie Rainey

Thanks for your faithful care and concern in beginning the process of building a healthy, growing self-esteem in each of us. We're proud to be your children.

CONTENTS

- You Are God's Arms of Love
- Esteem Builder Project

- Truth: A New Standard of Comparison
- Truth Is Powerful
- Truth Demands a Response
  - Law of Giving
  - Law of Understanding
  - Law of Perseverance
  - Law of Sowing and Reaping
  - Law of Teachability
  - Law of Accountability
  - Law of Risk
  - Law of God-Given Worth
  - Law of Divine Sufficiency
- Slaying the Phantom With the Truth
- The Building Blocks of Self-Esteem
- Esteem Builder Project

Building Block #1: Accepting Unconditionally

- Adam and Eve on Stage
- "Should We Keep Her?"
- God Speaks About Marriage — Leaving, Cleaving, and Becoming One Flesh
- The Great Mistake and What Happened Afterward
- Creating a Garden Experience in Your Marriage
- Making Acceptance Flourish
- What About Differences?
- Living With Your Mate's Differences
- Praying for Yourself
- Talking to Your Mate
- Tutor Your Mate With His Permission
- Ignoring Differences
- Continue to Verbalize Commitment
- Accept Your Mate Unconditionally
- Esteem Builder Project

Building Block #2: Putting the Past in Perspective

- The "Thing" in Dennis's Attic
- The Past and Your Mate's Self-Esteem
- The Dark Corner of Parents
- One Woman's Story

- Protect Your Wife
- Techniques to Honor Your Wife
- Hats a Wife Wears
- Develop Her Gifts and Horizons As a Woman
- Assist in Problem Solving
- Persevere With Your Investment
- Barbara's Tips to Men
- Esteem Builder Project

- The Collapsed Roof
- A Roof Is Like My Husband's Self-Esteem
- Choosing to Deny Yourself
- Understand His Manhood
- Give Him Total Acceptance
- Understand Our Male and Female Differentness
- Understand His Need For Work
- Understand His Sexual Need
- Benefits of Understanding
- Respect His Person
- Meet a Worthy Queen
- From the Palace of Persia to the Present
- Adapt to Him and Share His Dreams
- Esteem Builder Project

- The Twenty-Kilometer Walk
- Perseverance and Change
- Perseverance and Progress
- Perseverance and Purpose

FOREWORD

In the wake of a couple's marital spat, I was asked to give comfort to the shaken wife. Neighbors called the police; she called me. As I entered the home, I passed the departing patrolman who said, "It's just a matter of time — they need a divorce."

His conclusion grew out of reality: Half of all American marriages die in divorce courts. Many more hang together by thin, legal threads only. Weddings may be popular but marriages are *not* alive and well.

While the pessimistic percentages pass in review, a no-nonsense, self-help alternative has surfaced. With *Building Your Mate's Self-Esteem*, Dennis and Barbara Rainey have developed a kind of no-fault solution to the commonest irritant in the Mr. and Mrs. merger. They know the territory and they tackle the tough spots with realism and courage. Esteem Builder Projects and clarity of writing make this book an eloquent source of instruction — and review — for anyone seriously committed to a worthwhile marriage.

Dennis Rainey is no theorist. His Family Life Conferences nationwide have taught him to pick up the marital pulse accurately. He has been used by God as a powerful tool to impact homes and marriages as few men have. His principles are unerringly biblical yet up to speed for our urban pace. From the authenticity of their own relationship, Dennis and Barbara offer not just another book about marriage to set on the shelf, but rather an effective instrument which novice and veteran alike will find valuable.

Howard and Jeanne Hendricks
Dallas Theological Seminary

ACKNOWLEDGMENTS

Writing a book is enough of a challenge by itself. However, writing at home while faced with the reality of six children and a rapidly growing ministry means this book was a team effort.

Jeff Tikson has brought new meaning to the word "servanthood." You heroically supplied the leadership to solve a myriad of problems that surfaced while we were submerged in this book. Thanks, Jeff, you've become a trusted friend and co-laborer.

A special thanks to Lori Bricker for your care of our children. You deserve a medal of honor. We couldn't have done it without you.

The Family Ministry team deserves special commendation. You prayed, encouraged, pitched in, and supported us while faithfully carrying on the task of strengthening marriages and families. You all are a "Team of Destiny" — we've only just begun. Jerry Wunder, you are a gift from God — thanks for being a servant and giving leadership.

A special thanks goes to Fred Hitchcock for all his research and editing. Lynne Nelson, Jeff Lord and Sue Stinson all helped with the final manuscript.

Les Stobbe and Jean Bryant at HLP were two great coaches — thanks for being patient. Dan Benson and Gwen Waller were a big help in editing the ramblings of our typewriter. And thanks to Dennis Hensley who provided the training and encouragement we needed.

Craig Current, Joe Battaglia, Jane Ann Smith, Randy Marshall, Anne Crow, Dr. George Slaughter, Gay White and Steve Farrar — thanks to each of you for reading our "stuff " in its raw form and for giving us much-needed advice and balance. Thanks for being friends with a sharp pen.

Don and Sally Meredith have had and continue to have an immeasurable influence in our lives, marriage and ministry — thanks for discipling us in so many ways.

To our children — Ashley, Benjamin, Samuel, Rebecca, Deborah and Laura — THANK YOU! You are the most understanding and best children a pair of parents could ever hope to have. The little notes, cookies, hugs and prayers were more meaningful than you know. You are awesome!

INTRODUCTION

This is a book on motivating people to believe in people. Both you and your mate need to be believed in. Your mate needs at least one person in his life who will come alongside him and build him up. You are that person. And he is that person for you.

You ask, "Why is this so important?" The reason: We live in an era when personal sense of insecurity has reached near epidemic proportions. Confidence, true bedrock confidence, is rare. Even those people who appear to possess unshakeable self-esteem shock us with confessions of self-doubt. We're puzzled when we see so many high-performance people driven by poor self-esteem — people such as business leaders, speakers, pro athletes, entertainers, and even many Christian leaders.

Surprising as that is, it is in marriage that the "wraps of performance" really come off, revealing our mate's questions about his or her value and worth as a person. The beautiful or handsome, intelligent, gifted person we married admits deep feelings of insecurity. In fact, many people, when they marry, hope their mate will help them by doing the building and reshaping that they couldn't do for themselves.

A wife is stunned when she discovers that her husband, her "knight in shining armor," is really just an overgrown boy with serious questions about who he is as a man.

Or a husband begins to notice that the charming, poised woman who swept him off his feet is painfully insecure in relating to others.

When we marry, we take on the responsibility of helping secure and strengthen our mate's self-image. Unfortunately we are ill-equipped for such a complex task.

Our staff surveyed 17,000 marrieds and pre-marrieds at our Family Life Conferences by asking them, "In what area would you most like to have further training?" Rated number one by a wide margin, above finances, parenting, fathering, working women and others, was "How to Build Your Mate's Self-Esteem." That response confirmed the need for this book.

One of the leading authorities on the family, Dr. James Dobson, underscores the importance of building self-esteem in marriage.

> The most successful marriages are those where both husband and wife seek to build the self-esteem of the other. Ego needs can be met within the bonds of marriage, and nothing contributes more to closeness and stability than to convey respect for the personhood of the spouse.[1]

Not only does the success of your marriage depend on building your mate's self-esteem, but also your success in rearing children, and in life in general. Two confident partners will be much more effective in every aspect of life than two insecure people could ever be.

Let us outline five reasons we believe both you and your mate will benefit from this book:

1. It will help you focus on your mate's needs and not just your own. We know that you have needs in this area, too, but as you strengthen your mate's self-image, he will be increasingly free to give to you in return. Far too many marriages consist of two people who are waiting for each other to reach out and meet their needs.

2. Your mate may appear confident today — fully in charge of his life and capable of making wise decisions. But people change. Circumstances change. And changes will affect your mate. One wrong decision in the midst of these changes can crush a person's self-confidence. Your mate needs you to read this book and be able to apply its principles.

3. There is hope. God can and will produce growth in your mate's self-image. He still works in people's lives and He wants to use you. Far too many people underestimate their role in their mates' lives. They lose hope, and they give up too soon.

4. We believe that confident people ultimately can be released from preoccupation with self to becoming all that God designed them to be.

5. Although the practical principles found in our ten building blocks of self-esteem are written for marrieds, they also apply in our relationships with our children, our parents, our friends, and our associates at work. You'll be able to motivate others toward being all that God intended them to be as

you apply these basic truths.

The solutions we offer, however, are not the "cookie cutter" variety. Some may be intensely practical for you today, while others may require you to brush the dust off this book a decade from now. We are confident that the discoveries you are about to make can benefit you and your mate for years to come as you build each other's self-worth.

One last word. The Scriptures clearly teach that we are to edify one another. The word *edify* as used in the New Testament comes from two Greek words: *oikos,* which means "a home," and *dimeo,* which means "to build." Therefore, to edify literally means "to build a home." In the process of edifying your mate, a building is formed. As mentioned before, construction of your mate's self-esteem is not for his welfare alone. It will profit you, your children and others as well.

A NOTE TO OUR READERS

As writers, we face a dilemma. The English language does not contain a one-word equivalent for "he or she," yet we find it cumbersome to repeatedly refer to your mate as "he or she." Therefore, for the sake of readability, we generally will refer to your mate as "he."

— 1 —
Giving Your Mate a New Image

- Being Lovable Without Qualifying for Acceptance
- Your Mate's Mirror . . . Acceptance or Rejection?
- Strengthen Your Mate's Self-Image
- Love Casting Out Fear
- How Reality Tarnishes Self-Image
- The Natural Nature of Relationships
- Marriage Hasn't Failed . . . People Have Failed
- You Are Not Left Without Hope

HAVE YOU EVER been puzzled by your mate's lack of confidence, the evidence of weaknesses and flaws in his self-esteem? Have you asked yourself questions like:

Why is my husband driven toward accomplishment and achievement?

Why does my wife constantly compare herself with others?

Why is my husband so apathetic about life? Why is he so passive about trying anything new?

Why is my wife so indecisive?

Why does my husband find it so difficult to admit fault and ask for forgiveness?

Why is my wife so preoccupied with her past? With her failures and mistakes?

Why can't my husband relax? Why is he so guarded in relationships?

Why does my wife appear to be so solidly confident in so many areas of life and so filled with self-doubt in others?

All of these questions represent a deficiency or an erosion in self-confidence. Your mate may appear to have it all together, but you know, as few others do, that underneath that self-sufficient exterior lives a person who needs to be built up and encouraged repeatedly.

Because your mate has these weak spots, these "holes in his armor," he, like you, needs to be accepted unconditionally. He needs the security of knowing his wife accepts and believes in him, even when he doesn't believe in himself. And she needs the security of knowing that her husband knows her, yet won't reject her.

Each of us needs someone to tell us we are O.K. We need another person to give us a new image of ourself. We want to be accepted without mask, facade, or veneer. We want to be loved apart from our performance — totally and completely. As Maurice Wagner, author of two books on self-esteem, writes, "At the heart of personality is the need to feel a sense of being lovable without having to qualify for that acceptance."[1]

For your marriage to become a haven for your mate, you must accept him as he is, not for what you hope he will become.

She Loved Him for Who He Was

Dr. Paul Brand, chief of the rehabilitation branch of a leprosarium in southern Louisiana, knows of people's thirst for acceptance. Not only does he continue to see this need today among those with Hansen's disease, commonly known as leprosy, but he also has seen this need for acceptance in other places. He writes of his experience as a surgeon in London during World War II:

Peter Foster was a Royal Air Force pilot. These men [pilots] were the cream of the crop of England — the brightest, healthiest, most confident and dedicated, and often the most handsome men in the country. When they walked the streets in their decorated uniforms, the population treated them as gods. All eyes turned their way. Girls envied those who were fortunate enough to walk beside a man in Air Force blue.

However, the scene in London was far from romantic, for

the Germans were attacking relentlessly. Fifty-seven consecutive nights they bombed London. In waves of 250, some 1,500 bombers would come each evening and pound the city.

The RAF Hurricanes and Spitfires that pilots like Foster flew looked like mosquitoes pestering the huge German bombers. The Hurricane was agile and effective, yet it had one fatal design flaw. The single propeller engine was mounted in front, a scant foot or so from the cockpit, and the fuel lines snaked alongside the cockpit toward the engine. In a direct hit, the cockpit would erupt into an inferno of flames. The pilot could eject, but in the one or two seconds it took him to find the lever, heat would melt off every feature of his face: his nose, his eyelids, his lips, often his cheeks.

These RAF heroes many times would undergo a series of 20 to 40 surgeries to refashion what once was their face. Plastic surgeons worked miracles, yet what remained of the face was essentially a scar.

Peter Foster became one of those "downed pilots." After numerous surgical procedures, what remained of his face was indescribable. The mirror he peered into daily couldn't hide the facts. As the day for his release from the hospital grew closer, so did Peter's anxiety about being accepted by his family and friends.

He knew that one group of airmen with similar injuries had returned home only to be rejected by their wives and girlfriends. Some of the men were divorced by wives who were unable to accept this new outer image of their husbands. Some men became recluses, refusing to leave their houses.

In contrast, there was another group who returned home to families who gave loving assurance of acceptance and continued worth. Many became executives and professionals, leaders in their communities.

Peter Foster was in that second group. His girlfriend assured him that nothing had changed except a few millimeters' thickness of skin. She loved *him,* not his facial membrane, she assured him. The two were married just before Peter left the hospital.

"She became my mirror," Peter said of his wife. "She gave me a new image of myself. Even now, regardless of how I feel, when I look at her she gives me a warm, loving smile that tells me I am O.K.," he tells confidently.[2]

Mirrors of Acceptance

Did you know you are a mirror to your mate? You can either reflect the same loving acceptance Peter Foster's wife did, or you can withdraw from your mate, reflecting rejection.

When your mate looks into your face, his mirror, what does he see? If your mate sees rejection, or any lack of acceptance, the result will be fear. And that fear — the fear of rejection — is one of the most powerful forces motivating and controlling people today.

If you want to see your mate's self-image strengthened, then begin to recognize that the fear of rejection is your enemy. We read in 1 John 4:18, "Perfect love casts out fear." Fear will begin to dissolve in your mate under a steady stream of authentic love.

Give Your Mate the Gift of Value

Denis Waitley, in his book, *Seeds of Greatness,* underscores the poisonous effect of fear and the releasing power of love. He writes in his first chapter, "The Seed of Self-esteem":

> So then, the gift of value is the absence of fear. People who live with fear grow up standing at the end of every line. People who live with praise learn to stand alone and lead the parade, even if it's raining. People who are spoiled with indulgence and permissiveness grow up to be full of compromising greed. People who are given challenges and responsibilities grow up with values and goals. People who live with depression will need a drink, a puff, a pill to get them high; people who live with optimism will grow up thinking they were born to fly! People who live with hate grow up blind to beauty and true love. People who live with love, live to give their love away and are blind to hate. If our people are reminded of all the bad we see in them, they'll become exactly what we hoped they'd never be! But if we tell our people, "We're so glad you're in the game," they'll be glad to be alive, right now, and glad they wear their name.[3]

That's it — love casting out fear! Perfect love (God's love) is more powerful than the fear of rejection. Perfect love that accepts and embraces another, even in his weaknesses, will win the power struggle with fear every time. Rather than refuel the fear of rejection, you can remove it by accepting your mate.

But acceptance isn't always easy, as a young man in his mid-twenties and an attractive young lady discovered years ago.

What You See Is NOT All You Get

She was as smart as she was pretty. In fact, she was chosen as one of the university's "Top Twenty Freshmen Women."

As a child, this young lady received love and encouragement from her parents, and her family was esteemed by the community. Her parents modeled a stable marriage. There was little stress for her. Life seemed perfect . . . until she reached junior high.

While her other friends reached puberty quickly and began to develop physically, she did not. Her chest remained flat and her legs skinny, and her hips developed no contours.

Throughout the first six years of school, she had felt confident, sure of herself, popular. But as a seventh-grader who was slow to develop, she began to question her worth for the first time. This self-doubt was further fueled by her best friend who noticed her lack of "physical feminine maturity." One day this friend asked, "Are you sure you're a girl?"

Those words hit like a lightning bolt from an ominous dark cloud. Fear that she would never develop began to whisper in her inner spirit. Her personality changed. She became quiet, reserved, shy. Constantly comparing herself with others, she always came up short in her own eyes. She felt unpopular, unattractive and awkward, without personal value, and alone. And no one knew of her fears.

Finally, in her thirteenth year, she began to blossom. In fact, she became very pretty, yet inwardly she had developed a negative view of herself. Throughout high school she saw herself as inferior, and she thought everyone else saw her that way, too.

Determined to forge a new self-identity, the young woman decided to go to an out-of-state college where she could start fresh. She succeeded. Honor after honor came her way. She earned good grades, participated in numerous campus activities, and became very popular. In her sophomore year, she pledged one of the top sororities on campus.

Behind this newly found niche of success, however, was an insecure individual. She became an outstanding performer, yet no one, not even she, realized that at the heart of her performance was a little girl who was afraid to be known. The accomplishments gave her confidence a boost, but she still needed the acceptance of someone who really knew her. She needed to be accepted for who she was apart from her achievements.

One year after her college graduation, she fell in love with a young man who appeared to have it all together. He was the extroverted, confident person she was not. Their whirlwind romance found them married after only four months of dating.

She later found out that, although he was secure, he had needs, too. He was impulsive, brash and over-zealous. And behind his air of bravado and pride, he was hiding some insecurities of his own.

The Reality Hits Home

After nearly a month of marriage, both began to realize much more was going on inside each other than they had bargained for. One night, after an evening out with some friends, they stayed up talking about how inferior she felt in public settings. Her questions about her worth stunned him. He couldn't believe that this beautiful woman, his wife, could possibly feel that way about herself. He had absolute confidence in her.

After several of these late evening "chats," he finally realized his wife really did have some serious self-doubt. In fact, her withdrawn behavior at social gatherings began to irritate him. He silently questioned, *Why does she retreat into her protective shell of silence, when I feel so comfortable with people? Why can't she be like me?*

A Fork in the Road

That young couple was us more than fourteen years ago. At that time, we had critical choices to make. Would Dennis accept Barbara fully and love her during her periods of self-doubt? And would Dennis be vulnerable and risk being known by a young woman who might reject him? The choices were real. The decisions were tough. Fortunately, we made the right ones.

In retrospect, we believe those days were among the most crucial in our marriage. In those initial months, the foundations of acceptance and the patterns of response were laid.

As our fears and insecurities surfaced, we also discovered the critical importance of a healthy, positive self-concept to a marriage. We began to recognize the magnitude of the responsibility we each carried in building up or tearing down the other's self-esteem. And we both began to see that our own self-image either crippled or completed our marriage relationship.

The Natural Nature of Relationships

A letter that recently came across our desk further illustrates the need to build your mate's self-esteem. This wife and mother shared with us how her eight-year-old son brought healing to hurts her mate had caused.

> My son Benjie is such a leader and encouragement. Today is his birthday and he arranged for an old man who lives across the street to buy him a rose. He gave it to me tonight. When I asked what it was for, he replied, "Today is my birthday and I'm glad you're my Mom." Now you see what keeps me going — this little man in my life patches the breaks that the big man causes.

Here we see a woman who has experienced rejection, rather than acceptance, from her husband. Instead of her marriage strengthening her self-esteem, as God intended, her husband's contempt brought the need for an eight-year-old boy's thoughtful gesture of a rose.

Why aren't we better at building each other's self-esteem? Why is it so difficult to provide an atmosphere of acceptance for our mates? In seeking answers for these questions, we studied the conditions in our world which we believe are largely responsible for the present epidemic of poor self-esteem. Your mate's evaluation of his self-worth is affected by four current social trends.

1. A Self-Seeking Culture

We live in a culture of self-fulfillment. Modern men and women seem more focused on finding individual identity than at any point in history, yet to most people, a positive, healthy self-identity remains an elusive butterfly. We are a restless, self-indulgent society whose members often use each other to gain the acceptance they feel they deserve. Thus, we feel used and not genuinely needed, valued or appreciated. The sad admission of Christina Onassis, daughter of the Greek shipping magnate, Aristotle Onassis, illustrates this feeling of rejection:

"My most fervent wish is that I shall meet a man who loves me for myself and not my money."

People like Miss Onassis (and perhaps your mate) feel used because performance and possessions have become the ultimate measurement of worth and value. Society applauds people for what they have *done* and what they have *acquired* with seldom an ovation for who they *are*. Our culture says self-esteem is to be built on self-achievement. We feel we must be production-minded, so we generally don't cultivate the relationships that would foster feelings of lasting significance. As a result, we are being "driven" in the wrong direction by a wrong standard of value. (We will look at right values in chapter 4.)

2. Fractured Families

We live in a social structure that also is rocked (if not ripped apart) by divorce. If your mate's parents are not divorced, most likely someone else close to him is. You both certainly feel the effects of a nation plagued with a near 50 percent divorce rate. A Chinese proverb says, "In the broken nest there are no whole eggs." Broken homes generally do not produce whole people.

It's not that those who come from broken homes are not valuable or do not have great worth. They are, and they do. But much like an earthquake, a divorce is followed by years of emotional aftershocks — especially in the children. The tremors of fear, anger and guilt all rumble away, internally deteriorating a young person's self-image. He may have no idea for years how this broken relationship has created internal fissures and fractures in his identity.

Children are affected not only by legal divorce within the family, but by emotional divorce as well. Emotional divorce occurs when a husband and wife decide just to "live together," settling for a mediocre marriage. We believe this problem is much more extensive than divorce itself. Even some Christian marriages, it seems, are contaminated with dangerously low, nominal commitments. As a result, the children suffer — deeply.

3. The Fading of Dignity in Marriage

There is a growing disillusion with the dignity of marriage. The traditional marriage relationship is under attack and suspicion and our civil courts have reduced to rubble the nobility and sacredness of the marriage vows.

Because marriage has been robbed of the honor intended as indicated by the Scriptures, husbands and wives often feel they must look elsewhere for the personal fulfillment and encouragement that builds self-esteem. Yet marriage hasn't failed — people have. Because people have failed, marriage has received far too much "negative press." Many people have erroneously concluded that marriage itself is the culprit.

The perception of marriage as a consecrated estate has been tarnished by the views of others. One such view is that of Gloria Steinem, who has been an instigator of the attack on marriage. She says, "For the sake of those who wish to live in equal partnership, we must abolish and reform the institution of marriage." [4]

This philosophy can cause married couples to feel insignificant, as though they are trapped in a dying institution. The individual self-esteems of both you and your mate are bruised by these antagonistic ideologies.

4. *Unequipped Brides and Grooms*

No athletic team with good judgment would spend most of its budget, energy, or time on a magnificent pregame show, and little or none on training and preparation.

Yet couples today spend an inordinate amount of time and thousands of dollars on the wedding ceremony, and very little time and money, if any, on how to complete this cross-country run called marriage.

Thus, they are unequipped to meet the unique needs of their mates. Rather than being able to accept and build up their spouses, they generally are burdened by their own fears and insecurities. Under the influence of our culture, and carrying a self-image and value of marriage largely determined by parents, these men and women march off into lifelong relationships with a partner who is equally ill-prepared.

Weighted down by the past and confused by the culture, these young couples are increasingly unqualified to deal with the complex issues surrounding their mates' needs for self-worth. The following story illustrates what can happen when they face these issues unprepared.

A Model Christian Couple?

By all outward appearances, Laura and Mark were a model couple. With an apparently happy marriage, they enjoyed the benefits of social acceptance in one of the most prestigious neighborhoods in the city, an enormously successful business, and three beautiful, healthy children. The wall of protection around their lives was their personal, balanced involvement in an outstanding church. Nothing was missing. Everything seemed to be going their way.

So, imagine our shock when Laura sought us out for help. She described her life and their marriage as a "mockery." "We have no relationship," she said. "We can't relax. And the only thing we ever talk about is his business.

"I feel Mark is committed to the marriage, but not to me. He just doesn't want to take on any responsibility at home, especially when it comes to me and my needs.

"I have a growing bitterness toward his work. I see him giving the best of his leadership there. Organizing, planning and motivating people . . . he's the best. But at home it's another matter. And with me, well, I feel he is growing indifferent. I feel terribly insecure because I don't feel he needs me. As a result, I've grown very critical of him, and of everything he does."

Later, I (Dennis) spent some time with Mark, who admitted he had not made his marriage a priority. "I never tore her down — I guess I just neglected her. I didn't see why I should open up to her with my problems, because she has her own problems. I've been in the process of getting my business settled and then, after we were set financially, I was planning to cash in on my family." With a despairing shrug, he added, "Suddenly, it dawned on me there wasn't going to be any relationship at home. I wouldn't have my wife to fall back on.

"As time went on, I grew more and more independent. We became isolated. I watched Laura become fearful and very insecure. She was scared to death and I wasn't certain I knew how to deal with all of her newly developed insecurities. Her shaky confidence began to infect me. I began to feel shackled by her clingy dependence and need for approval. She became a weight instead of a wife. I lost all desire to build her up."

Mark concluded, "I realize now that our marriage license did not make a marriage. It only gave us the *right* to begin building one."

Laura summed up her feelings, "We're just two outwardly successful people doing our own thing, but independent of one another. *Our marriage consists of each of us trying to get the other to meet our own needs, each waiting for the other to take the first step."*

Building Your Mate

In these confessions of a successful twentieth-century couple, we find the wife saying, "He's committed to the marriage, but not to me," and "I don't feel needed." Then the husband said, "I didn't see why I should open up to her with my problems . . . she had enough of her own," and "I wasn't sure I knew how to deal with her fears." These admissions are like windows, letting us peek into an outwardly strong house to see the insecurity, fear and isolation inside. Sadly, many have come to accept these feelings in marriage as a part of life — like the common cold.

This scene is being played over and over and over, like a scratched record, in thousands of Christian marriages today. Perhaps you, like both of us, entered marriage plagued by some degree of personal self-doubt and insecurity, but carefully masked it behind performance and intense romantic feelings. When your mate's weaknesses surfaced, you felt overwhelmed and at a loss as to what to do.

Often, couples instinctively turn *on* each other, rather than courageously turning *to* each other to seek to build confidence and security. Instead of the marriage relationship being a haven in the storm, it becomes the storm itself. Pounded and drenched on the outside by the continual downpour of society's attacks, it now faces a problem of flooding from within. With both partners insecure in their self-esteem and afraid to reach out, they retreat and wait. Unfortunately, many of these marriages ultimately drown and become statistics in the divorce court, and far too many Christian marriages settle for a "negotiated and friendly" emotional divorce.

A Message With Hope

Snoopy, the cherished Peanuts cartoon pet, sat droopy-eyed at the entrance of his dog house. He lamented, "Yesterday I was a dog. Today I'm a dog. Tomorrow I'll probably still be a dog. SIGH. There's so little hope for advancement!"

Perhaps you feel like Snoopy — hopeless, with very little expectation of any change in your mate or yourself. "SIGH.

There's no hope for my mate in this area." Or, "I'll always be a human with these limitations."

You may think your mate's self-image is like permanently hardened cement. It can change, however. Cement can be broken out and repoured, but it takes your diligence.

There is hope. Failures, past and present, can be overcome. That is one of the encouragements for us as Christians. There is always the potential for change. God has not left us without hope or power, drifting aimlessly. The Scriptures offer a powerful promise: "For nothing will be impossible with God."[5]

That's exactly what we've experienced in our marriage! Growth and hope. Though it's been difficult at times, we wouldn't trade the growth we've seen in each other's lives for any other satisfaction.

You and your mate *can* experience that, too. We believe your marriage, like ours, provides one of the best possible relationships in which two people can build the self-image of each other. The ten building blocks we will share with you will give you the practical help you've needed to see your mate's confidence quotient soar. But first you must understand how your mate established his self-esteem.

To discover how effectively biblical principles apply to improving your own self-image, see Josh McDowell's *His Image . . . My Image.*[6]

— 2 —
Slaying the Phantom

EARLY ON A CRISP September morning in 1944, two cyclists taking cover in a small French town near the Luxembourg border decided that it was safe at last to venture out into the countryside. . . . The nighttime rumble of tanks had died away. So the men mounted up and swept along the road that passed the bivouac. They sniffed the smoke of cooking fires in the cold autumn air. They noted the usual scattering of grimy, mud-stained vehicles, partly hidden under tattered camouflage nets: a couple of trucks, some trailers and a few big M-4 tanks with their mighty guns poking out from the cover of trees and netting.

Then, a young American sentry stopped the pair. He was friendly enough, but firm. They must explain where they were going and why. The Frenchmen replied as well as they could until, all at once, they stiffened and fell silent, their eyes wide

in astonishment. For over the sentry's shoulder they saw four
GIs in muddy battle jackets and dull-green helmets walk over
to a monstrous tank and, with one man at each corner, simply
pick it up, turn it around and set it down again. Thus . . .
was the cover of the 603rd Engineer Camouflage Battalion broken and the security of a neighboring armored division imperiled
at a critical moment in the Allied offensive. Fortunately, no
damage was done.

The 603rd was one of four units that formed what was
perhaps the most enigmatic outfit ever fielded in battle, a group
called the 23rd Headquarters Special Troops. The 23rd's troops
were "special" all right. They specialized in impersonating other
troops. . . . With inflatable rubber guns and vehicles, with
ever-changing shoulder patches, stencils to make phony signs,
and with amplified recordings of heavy equipment in action,
the 23rd played role after role. . . .

The purpose of all that razzle-dazzle was to fool the enemy
and, by doing so, enable the troops that the 23rd was impersonating to sneak into new positions, to launch a surprise attack or
in some other way to catch the other side off guard.[1]

Forty years ago this phantom division played a role in
Germany's defeat. With careful staging and show-business theat-
rics, they impersonated real troops and created an illusion of
military strength. The Germans were fooled and confused. The
23rd was successful.

"Confused" and "fooled" may describe what your mate
feels today when he thinks about himself, his identity and the
roles he must play. Unsure of the answers to basic questions
such as "Who am I?" and "Am I important or valuable?" your
mate, as the German army in World War II, may be deceived
by phantoms, and therefore is not living successfully as God
intended.

What Is a Phantom?

A phantom is an unattainable mental image or standard
by which we measure our performance, abilities, looks, character
and life. It is perfect, idyllic. A phantom, by definition, is an
illusion, an apparition, or a resemblance of reality. Disguised
as the truth, its distortion is exposed only through a careful,
unhurried, unhindered inspection.

A multitude of phantoms lurks in the minds of men and
women. There is the phantom husband or wife, the phantom

father or mother, the phantom family, job or friend. We all have them.

Barbara's phantom is the perfect wife, mother and friend, always loving, patient, understanding and kind. She is well-organized, with a perfect balance between being disciplined and flexible. Her house is always neat and well-decorated, and her children obey the first time, every time. She is serious yet lighthearted, submissive but not passive. She is energetic and never tired. She looks fresh and attractive at all times, whether in jeans and a sweater digging in the garden or in a silk dress and heels going to dinner. She never gets sick, lonely or discouraged. And because her phantom is a Christian, Barbara sees her faithfully walking with God daily. This phantom prays regularly, studies diligently and is not fearful or inhibited about sharing her faith or speaking the truth to someone who may be in error.

Dennis's phantom is just as idyllic. He rises early, has a quiet time reading the Bible and praying, and then jogs several seven-minute miles. After breakfast with his family, he presents a fifteen-minute devotional. Never forgetting to hug and kiss his wife good-bye, he arrives at work ten minutes early. He is consistently patient with his co-workers, always content with his job, and has problem-solving techniques for every situation. At lunch he eats only perfectly healthful foods. His desk is never cluttered, and he is confidently in control. He arrives home on time every day and never turns down his boys when they want to play catch.

His phantom is well-read in world events, politics, key issues of our day, the Scriptures and literary classics. He's a handy-man around the house and loves to build things for his wife. He is socially popular and never tires of people or of helping them in time of need. He obeys all traffic laws and never speeds, even if he's late. He can quote large sections of Scripture in a single bound, has faith more powerful than a locomotive, and is faster than a speeding bullet in solving family conflicts. He never gets discouraged, never wants to quit, and always has the right words for every circumstance. He also keeps his garage neat. He never loses things, always flosses his teeth and has no trouble with his weight. And he has time to fish.

The Origins of Phantoms

Where do phantoms come from? They don't appear overnight, as the American 23rd battalion did. Each phantom slowly grows from the seeds of our individual experience. Ours came from expectations placed on us by parents, peers, employers, coaches, and teachers in school and Sunday school.

Dorothy Corkille Briggs, in her classic work, *Your Child's Self-Esteem,* said, "Children rarely question [their parents'] expectations; instead, they question their personal adequacy."[2] Like a child with his parents, your mate typically doesn't question the phantom. Innocently, he accepts the lofty standards and ideals of the phantom just as he accepted his parents' standards and expectations when he was a little child.

Phantoms, with their unattainable attributes, also can develop as your mate compares his or her life with others. These faulty comparisons can be fueled by a friend, employer, or even by you.

We can be like Lucy, who said one day to her famous cartoon buddy, "You are a foul ball in the line drive of life, Charlie Brown!" Making comparisons with what we feel is normal and acceptable only makes the unattainable phantom more intimidating. Because he doesn't always compare favorably, your mate concludes that he is a foul ball.

Perhaps your wife watches people she admires and assigns those character and personality traits, abilities and talents she envies most to her growing, changing phantom. She also may observe the negative side of other women and conclude, "I will never do that or be that way." Another standard, that of never failing, is added to the phantom.

The problem of your mate comparing his life with another is that it ordinarily is done from a distance and when the other person is generally at his best. Since your mate is acutely aware of his own flaws and shortcomings, he further depreciates his own value when focusing on the apparent best of the other person. Consequently, your mate is destined to feel like a loser even though he may be a winner in many areas of his life. It is impossible to compare without lowering self or another.

Your mate's phantom, the result of his comparisons and others' expectations, is unreachable, so your mate experiences failure. These failures stand tall in the corridors of your mate's mind, continually reminding him of his deficiencies.

These failures added together with his successes in life produce another mental concept, called your mate's self-image.

What Is a Self-Image?

Self-image, self-esteem, self-concept — three terms used to describe not only how your mate mentally *sees* himself, but how he *feels* about himself and what value and sense of worth he has internally.

Norman Wright, in his book, *Improving Your Self-Image,* writes, "The image we have of ourself is built upon clusters of many memories."[3] Each of us has developed this image over time. Norman Wright goes on to say, "Very early in life we begin to form concepts and attitudes about ourself, other people, and the world. Our self-concept is actually a cluster of attitudes about ourself — some favorable and some unfavorable."[4]

Like a police department's composite sketch of a criminal suspect, your mate's self-esteem is a composite drawing acquired from various sources and firsthand accounts. Countless sources over many years have contributed to his artistic rendering of self.

A Portrait With Music

But the drawing is not silent. A self-image isn't just what your mate thinks about himself, but it contains what he feels about himself, too. It is not a black and white, one-dimensional, charcoal sketch. It is a full-color, three-dimensional painting with feelings, a portrait with stereophonic music.

What kind of self-portrait has your mate painted? What kind of music does he hear? Do you really know? When the music of self-doubt is not playing, your mate feels confident, secure, relaxed. But when the voice and emotions of failure blare in your mate's ears, the self-condemnation can cause paralysis. Feelings of tension, fear and insecurity can control the way he thinks about himself and his life. Are you aware of what causes these feelings in your mate's life?

Perhaps, however, your mate is so "steady" that you rarely see him vacillate between confidence and insecurity. The temptation is to assume he hears no negative music. But your mate may have learned early in life to compensate for feelings of inadequacy by covering them with the appearance that all is well. Inside he has become accustomed to hearing the condemning music, but he rarely lets you know how he truly feels. Afraid of the rejection of others, he listens to the monotonous, accusing music alone. Outwardly, his performance may even be flawless, as though he had no needs. Inwardly, however, his secret inner desire is to have you rescue him by taking the needle off the negative recording and replacing the record with pleasant music that says "well done" or "you are accepted as you are." His real need is to be built up and loved for who he is.

We cannot divorce these two: what he thinks about himself (his self-portrait) and his feelings about himself (the accompanying music). They are inseparably linked. They are your mate's self-image. He lives with the music playing and the painting in place. It hangs in the museum of his mind and emotions as either a collector's item, priceless and original, or as a cheap imitation, accompanied with feelings of worthlessness and insignificance.

The Centrality of Self-Image

Your mate's self-image is central to all he is and does daily. In *Seeds of Greatness* Denis Waitley calls our self-esteem "the beginning and first seed to all success. It is the basis for our ability to love others and to try to accomplish a worthy goal, without fear."[5] Your mate's self-esteem will either hinder or enhance his ability to learn, make decisions, take risks and resolve conflicts with you and others. It will either restrain him or refuel him.

Yet, in spite of its importance, your mate may not understand how his self-esteem colors all that he does: his behavior, his relationships and his performance. For some it is painful even to admit they have needs in this area. But they do have needs. Your mate needs you.

Thomas Fuller said, "A danger foreseen is half avoided." Certainly, admitting your self-image inadequacies to one another is the beginning step to real healing and new intimacy in your marriage.

Your Mate Needs You

Your mate, like the Germans, may have lived for years under the looming shadow of the phantom. Possibly both of you have begun to perceive how the imposter has masqueraded as a reality in your lives, intimidating you almost daily. This, coupled with painful experiences, often results in a poor self-image.

Your mate needs your objective eye, talented paintbrush, and listening ear to help affirm him when he is O.K., and to correct him when he is in error. Some of the ideals your mate has lumped together in the phantom may not be bad standards. Your mate may merely need your help in balancing the demands of life with those ideals.

The "Esteem Builder Project" at the end of this chapter will assist you in helping your mate slay the phantom and replace negative experiences and images with positive ones. The following two chapters will provide foundational help in building your mate's self-esteem. Chapter 3, "Detecting the Clues," will strengthen your understanding of why your mate acts the way he does. Chapter 4, "Nine Laws That Liberate," will provide some universal precepts that will give you hope as you begin setting your mate free from the shackles of a poor self-image.

ESTEEM BUILDER PROJECTS: ESSENTIAL TO APPLICATION

"The object of Bible study is changed lives. The Christian world is suffering from a deficiency of Vitamin *A* — Application."

— Dr. Howard G. Hendricks
Dallas Theological Seminary

The objective of this book is to build marriages, not minds. There is a tendency to assume that learning facts and gaining knowledge is the solution, but marriages are built by couples who *apply God's Word together.*

Our hope is that you will convert God's truth into godly behavior. *Building Your Mate's Self-Esteem* is packed with knowledge and information, but your marriage will benefit only if you incorporate the truths into your daily life. We have attempted to emphasize a healthy balance between instruction and application by including "Esteem Builder Projects" at the conclusion of nearly every chapter.

The object is to make your marriage all that God intended it to be. These projects are a critical part of that process. Commit yourselves to interact on these projects, and you are sure to build your mate's self-esteem.

ESTEEM BUILDER PROJECT
(Use a sheet of paper if necessary.)

1. Explain to your mate the concept of the phantom, and then ask him to describe his own ideal man (or woman). Jot down his descriptions and discuss them. Which ones are appropriate and worth working to achieve? Which ones are unrealistic?
2. How is the phantom a real enemy to be dealt with in your mate's life? How has the phantom affected your mate's self-esteem? Ask your mate how he wants you to help him when his phantom is on parade. Discuss as a couple.
3. Ask your mate to describe what he thinks and how he feels about himself. Record the words he uses. Which are "thinking" words and which are "feeling" words? Any clues here to the impact of his phantom on his self-image?
4. Ask your mate to give you one way you can be a completer, not a crippler, of his self-esteem. What does he *need* you to do today?

— 3 —
Detecting the Clues

- Clues of an Inadequate Self-Esteem
- Ten Clues to Understanding the Condition of Your Mate's Self-Esteem
  - Family Background Affects Who We Are
  - Fear of Being Vulnerable
  - A Pattern of Discouragement
  - Lack of Confidence in Decision Making
  - Difficulty Admitting Wrong; Unable to Forgive
  - Driven to Be a High Achiever
  - Critical of Others
  - Perfectionist
  - Self-Depreciation
  - Escaping From the Real Issues of Life
- You Are God's Arms of Love
- Esteem Builder Project

AS A YOUNG GIRL, one of my (Barbara's) favorite pastimes was reading books. I spent several summers inching my way up a thermometer in my local library's book-reading contest. Often my mother found me curled up in a hand-me-down chair, or nestled in a corner halfway up the carpeted stairs, with my nose in a book. I was hopelessly lost in those pages, imagining myself a player in the unfolding drama. I didn't like coming back to reality. It was much too boring compared to the adventures of Nancy Drew.

I followed Nancy on most of her heroic adventures and grew in appreciation of the fine art of careful observation and cautious conclusion-drawing. Other renowned sleuths, such as Sherlock Holmes and, more recently, Agatha Christie's Miss

41

Marple and Hercule Poirot, are famous because of their eye for detail. They always seem to find the clues needed to solve the mystery.

Just as those "super sleuths" look beyond the obvious for hints, so you too must learn to piece together the hidden and ambiguous clues, along with those your mate conspicuously reveals, to solve the mystery of where and how to build his self-esteem.

Becoming a detective does not require donning a khaki trench coat with turned-up collar, and tiptoeing around with a magnifying glass. But it does require some training in observation. We need to learn to look and listen, to evaluate the evidence at hand, and to search for the hidden clues. These clues lead us to information that is critical in building our mate's self-esteem.

CLUES OF AN INADEQUATE SELF-ESTEEM

Silently lurking in the closets and attic of your mate's past and present life are dozens of clues signaling insecurity, fearfulness, or low self-confidence, which all result from poor self-esteem. You probably already have recognized that your mate has needs in this area, or you wouldn't be reading this book. This chapter will help you better understand your mate and build in the areas where he needs it most.

The following ten clues will help you understand the origins of your mate's phantom and the experiences that helped shape his self-esteem. Look closely and listen carefully, for your mate's sake.

Your mate's childhood was marked by parental abuse, parental neglect, parental ignorance, or parents with overbearing authority.

What is your mate's family background? Did his father and mother clearly love each other and their children? Was your mate encouraged as a child? Did his parents instill confidence and a sense of worth and value? Did they believe in him and express it frequently?

Parade magazine featured an interview with comedian Steve Allen and his wife, Jayne Meadows, on their many years together in marriage. Much of the article focuses on Steve's unstable family background. In a final comment about his childhood, Jayne said, "We are who we are because of where we've been."[1]

Steve Allen is who he is today because he came from a family of cynics on the vaudeville circuit. He was left alone and often neglected. He learned to use his natural sense of humor to cover up his deep loneliness and feelings of rejection. Allen's life illustrates the truth that our background largely determines what we will become in our personalities and, more important, in our self-esteems.

Your mate's self-esteem is a result of where he's been, too. His parents may have been too permissive, too smothering, too strict, too "religious," or worse yet, abusive or neglectful. Imagine what your spouse's life was like growing up. How did he feel? How would you have felt?

If his parents are still living, listen carefully to the way they communicate with their child as an adult. It may be different, but chances are the patterns of relating are still intact.

Encourage your mate as you begin to learn about his home life. Empathize with him and tell him it hurts you, too, that he experienced emotional pain as a child. Your husband or wife needs you to listen and care. But be careful not to become critical of his parents or peers for what they did or did not do. Blaming others does not relieve the problem; it increases it. It adds the burden of a resentful spirit, which can enslave you and your mate. Give his parents the benefit of the doubt. Assume they did the best they could with what they knew.

 Your mate fears opening up, being real, and being vulnerable with you and with others.

Fear is usually embedded in a poor self-esteem. We fear a host of things, yet for many the greatest is the fear of rejection. For example, your mate may fear failing, or appearing stupid, forgetful or insensitive, or numerous other things. All of these can become grounds for rejection by another, usually someone important or close to him.

The more fears your mate has, the less open he will be in a relationship. If the words *withdrawn* and *unexpressive* describe your mate, that's a clue to his insecurity — the blight of actual or perceived rejections in his past. Your mate is fearful of being known and afraid of being rejected.

Be careful of communicating rejection to your mate in any way, especially if he's not naturally transparent. He may be trying to open up, yet you may fuel the rejection he fears. Instead, seek to understand him. Ask yourself, "Why is my mate fearful?" Maybe he feels he tried to be open and it didn't work; he felt misunderstood. So he's given up. You may need to ask his forgiveness for adding to his fearful thoughts.

What a fearful person needs most from his mate is to be received gently in love when he attempts to express himself. He needs to be listened to. Recognize that his fears are real, no matter how inconsequential they may seem to you. To be ignored makes him feel uncared for and unimportant.

James 1:19 says it this way: "Let every one be quick to hear, slow to speak and slow to anger." Great advice for all, but especially for the marriage partner who tends to talk rather than listen.

In marriage, a delicate balance between being open and stopping to listen must be maintained. The climate of acceptance should be such that each partner feels free to share his thoughts, feelings and questions without fear of rejection.

If your mate is fearful, it is your responsibility to create quiet, non-threatening, unhurried times for the two of you to be together. Don't fear silence. When your mate does open up, listen and ponder his words. Think about your reply before you give it, and thank him for what he shared with you. You may have no idea how deep-seated and painful his fears really are.

 Your mate gets discouraged easily.

A mate who is easily discouraged is communicating, "I don't have confidence in my ability. I'm afraid I'll fail. So if I don't try, I won't experience defeat."

What this person needs is a loving, understanding cheerleader to come alongside him and believe the best. As you support your mate, ask questions to help you discover what discourages him and why this pattern is a part of his life. What real or imagined failures in your mate's experiences have led him to develop this facet of his self-esteem?

 Your mate lacks confidence, especially in decision making.

Making decisions, especially the critical ones, is difficult for anyone, but for some it can be excruciating. A person with large doses of self-doubt rarely trusts his own judgment in decision making. Perhaps many decisions were made for him by over-controlling parents, and he never developed a track record of trust in his own decision-making ability. Possibly he was derided for poor decisions and early in life chose to let others decide for him.

Regardless, decision making in any area becomes risky when a person has self-doubt and little confidence. Frequently he becomes a follower and finds safety and security in flowing with the crowd.

Here is an opportunity to observe and understand sympathetically so you can come alongside him and begin to rebuild the crumbled wall of confidence. Don't rush in and make all his decisions for him, rescuing him from the pain and, therefore, the risk of a wrong decision. Encourage him to decide and help him in the process. When he is thinking clearly and headed for an accurate decision, verbally praise him for his insight and reasoning. If he makes a poor decision, don't chide him or reject his efforts. Tell him you're proud that he stepped out and decided. Put his decision in perspective. Most decisions are not irreversible or life-threatening.

Above all, be patient. A person who does not feel competent in the decision-making process will take an inordinate amount of time to decide. Until he has a track record of good choices and feels good about himself, you can expect the process to take some time. You may need to remind him that to make no decision is often worse than making the wrong decision. Above all, permit your mate the room to make wrong decisions.

Your mate has difficulty admitting he is wrong, always needs to be right, or is unable to forgive.

We may mentally label this mate as prideful or arrogant, but rarely do we see him as being insecure. Pride gives the air of confidence and great ability.

But this person is like a sheep in wolf's clothing. His inability to admit mistakes and ask forgiveness is a mask of protection covering a fearful creature. Rather than hide his low self-esteem by being a follower, this individual projects the "take-charge, confident" exterior he wishes were true internally.

Samuel Butler said, "There is no mistake so great as that of being always right." If your mate has a need always to be right, you know the truth of that statement. It's tough to live with someone like this and it can create in you a growing feeling of not being able to measure up or of always being wrong.

Give your mate freedom to be who he is. Ask God to give you sympathetic understanding. Maybe as a child, your mate was always told he was wrong, even when he wasn't. Perhaps he felt inferior or bullied by an older brother or sister. Alone and feeling unworthy, consciously or subconsciously, he may have said, "Someday I won't have to be wrong anymore." Perhaps your mate feels that to be wrong is to be a failure, and to admit that is simply too threatening to his "needy" ego.

Also give your mate unconditional acceptance. Never correct him publicly or in front of your children. Be sensitive and advise him privately. He won't feel nearly as threatened with just you. And pray that God will use you to help soften him.

 Your mate is a driven person.

"Being driven" is widely used today to describe individuals who are outwardly high achievers because they are driven inwardly by a deep need for approval. It's a growing problem in our fast-paced culture. The television commercial that shows the investments man up late at night and up before dawn the next morning "working for you" projects an image of success and prosperity. Another advertisement shows perfectly dressed young urban professionals dashing in and out of taxis, glancing at their watches, looking like VIPs. These vignettes subtly communicate what the insecure person wants most — a sense of importance, of being needed, of having value.

This inner need for significance and personal worth causes people to be driven. They are seeking to gain their value as men or women through performance, whether it be in the arena of politics, career, athletics, the ministry or motherhood.

Many who have achieved "financial success" still feel they have a long way to go. J. D. Rockefeller, when asked how much money would be enough for him, replied, "One more dollar than I have." Something kept driving him to earn more money, but he never felt satisfied.

The symptoms of this common affliction are constant activity, endless meetings, appointments and counseling, and emergencies only the driven person can handle. The driven man or woman is habitually over-scheduled and usually afraid to say no. Because he gains his importance from others, he becomes a slave to others' opinions. Security and significance are to be earned by performance. The driven person won't stop and rest or think. Relationships suffer because there is no time. His life is unbalanced.

Driven people seek the praise of others to affirm their own worth. The problem is, they usually get it. But that acceptance is based on performance and production. It's what they do that counts, not who they are. The more they do, the more praise they receive. But as Sidney Harris says, "Self-achievement is no guarantee of self-acceptance."

If your mate is driven or has tendencies to be driven, what he needs most is your acceptance and praise for who he is as a person, apart from his performance. Don't become part of the problem by kindling your mate's need to perform. If you give acceptance and praise only when he does well and succeeds, and you communicate discouragement at failures, then you are telling your mate he is acceptable only when he performs and achieves (which is what he has been telling himself for years).

He needs you to bring balance to a life that is most likely out of control. Help him with his scheduling. Help him say *no* at least once a day. Help him understand how continual over-commitments only increase his chances of failure and can add to his feelings of inadequacy.

 Your mate is critical of others.

If your mate tends to be critical of others, if he frequently passes judgment on how things are done or handled, it's another clue of a poor self-esteem. Hiding behind this critical spirit is a self-image trying to lift itself up by pulling others down. It says, "My idea was better," "My way would have worked," "I could have done a better job if I'd had the chance," or "They don't ever do things right." These thoughts and comments are your mate's attempts to give value to his inner person at the expense of others.

Help your mate by being on his team but not taking sides. Be a coach to encourage him. Help him see the other side without defecting to the other team. And don't join him in becoming critical. He doesn't need you to tear others down, too. That doesn't build his self-esteem; it only encourages a weakness.

 Your mate is a perfectionist.

Modern psychology documents that most first-borns are perfectionists. So also are many second- and third-born children because, as Dr. W. Hugh Missildine says in *Your Inner Child of the Past,* perfectionism "literally runs in families."[2]

A perfectionist is compelled to have things just so, perfectly ordered. He tends to be inflexible with himself and others. He works hard and accomplishes much, but is rarely satisfied with his work or himself.

He is looking for acceptance, and thereby inner tranquility, by striving for perfection. But this orderly life usually eludes him. Because of his high standards, he is especially enslaved to a mental phantom of what he should be. Some have such perfectionistic standards that if they perform up to the qualifications of their phantom, they quickly raise the standard even higher. They create an "ultra phantom" in one area of their lives and call themselves failures for not achieving it.

Your mate may be too concerned about orderliness, correct grammar, personal appearance and beauty, home decorating, hard work, or financial success. Many of the world's most beautiful people are inwardly the most insecure. Women whose homes are perfectly clean and look like they came out of the pages of *House Beautiful* often apologize when you drop in because "the house is a mess."

Perfectionists have difficulty savoring the satisfaction of a job well done. They always think, "I could have done better," or "I didn't try hard enough." And they sometimes mistrust the authentic praise of others.

Does your mate see himself as a failure in some area, even though outwardly you and others think he's doing a good job? Does he have areas in which he pushes himself and other areas that don't seem to matter as much?

Once again, understanding will allow you to see in your mate a child who was not given complete approval, but was told, "That's nice, but you can do better. Why don't you try again?" Most likely he grew up feeling like a failure academically, physically, athletically, socially, or in whatever area complete approval was withheld. Your mate rarely enjoyed the solid satisfaction of a job well done.

Help your mate believe the truth: that his accomplishments are excellent and that he can do well. Encourage him to relax even though everything is not perfectly ordered. Stop and enjoy his accomplishments with him. Together, seek to understand "where he's been" to unlock the "why" behind his present behavior.

 Your mate is critical of self.

Closely akin to perfectionism is the voice of self-depreciation. Continually criticizing himself, the mate who harbors a poor self-esteem is desperately seeking approval. Just as this need for approval is the force behind a perfectionist's high standards and hard work, so this same need is the source of endless, varied negative comments about himself. Statements such as, "I can't do anything right," "I'm not very talented," or "I'm not very good at . . ." are clues.

Other signals sent through the fog of bad feelings about self are "fishing for compliments" statements. Your mate may ask, "Do you like the way I look in my new dress?" or "How do you like the way I fixed my office?" Are those the real questions? Is your mate looking for your objective opinion? Or is he looking for more? Is your mate secretly hoping for a dose of genuine approval?

Another sign of self-depreciation is difficulty receiving gifts and compliments. If your mate doesn't feel worthy as a person, he won't feel worthy of gifts, either material or verbal. He will somehow belittle the gift to make it more appropriate, saying something like, "You shouldn't have," or "This is too much." He might respond to a compliment with, "That's not true," or "You don't really mean that."

Perhaps your mate is self-conscious. He tends to wonder what others are thinking about him. He imagines that all eyes are focused on him, and he fears he will stumble. He questions his appearance, his conversational skills, and his mannerisms. He may be acutely aware of every physical blemish he has.

Gently correct your mate's inaccurate self-assessments. You may grow weary of hearing his negative thoughts about himself, but continue to accept him, affirm him and praise him for who he is.

Your mate needs to know that those physical things he doesn't like about himself don't matter to you, and the personality or character qualities he dislikes don't affect your love and acceptance of him as a person of worth. Offer to help your mate in areas he doesn't like that do need to change, but never withhold genuine acceptance. Your mate's self-esteem will never grow without it.

 Your mate indulges in escapism.

The other day a bumper sticker caught our attention:
REALITY IS FOR THOSE WHO CAN'T COPE WITH DRUGS

This is a sad reflection of our culture today. We have learned to avoid facing the real issues in life through various means of escape. Your mate may escape from reality through drugs, alcohol, food, or even the pursuit of material possessions.

Fearful of having to deal with inconsistencies, personality defects, character flaws, or just plain pressure, too many people escape to the world of fantasy. They become alien to the real world, denying its realities and responsibilities. They create a fictitious image of themselves that never fails and never lets others down. In this state of denial they live and take up citizenship.

Without question, this is one of the most difficult coping mechanisms to deal with. The real world of responsibility, pain and pressure does not offer the lure and deceptive promise that fantasy does.

You must gently bring your mate to the point where he sees that an escape from reality is actually a decision to quit. Organizations that deal with alcoholism and drug dependency may be helpful, and perhaps even necessary.

Offer your mate a real relationship with a real person and real benefits. Do not underestimate the power of love in bringing another person back from these fantasies.

You Are God's Arms of Love

Having uncovered the telltale fingerprints and shrouded evidence of the past, do you feel you have your work cut out for you? Do you feel you have a mountain to climb or only a small hill?

Hebrews 12:12,13 tells us what to do next: "Therefore, strengthen the hands that are weak and the knees that are feeble, and make straight paths for your feet, so that the limb which is lame may not be put out of joint, *but rather be healed*" (italics added).

Are your mate's hands or knees weak? Or is he lame? Part of God's design for our marriage and yours is that we each be built up and made strong. You are God's physical arms of love and acceptance to your mate.

ESTEEM BUILDER PROJECT
(Use a sheet of paper if necessary.)

1. Pick (isolate) one or two obvious clues that signal insecurity in your spouse. List what evidence led you to those clues. What can you begin doing in each area to help create an environment for growth?
2. If you and your mate are reading this book together, discuss which clues best describe yourself and what you would suggest your mate do to help build your self-esteem.
3. Take a self-esteem inventory with your mate, using the accompanying form. You may photocopy it if you like.

SELF-ESTEEM INVENTORY

A. Read through this list of descriptions. Using the following scale, rate yourself, then ask your mate to rate himself for each description:

U = Usually   S = Sometimes   R = Rarely

Self	DESCRIPTION	Mate
_____	Fears change	_____
_____	Is introspective	_____
_____	Fears rejection	_____
_____	Seeks to identify with accomplishments	_____
_____	Is critical of self	_____
_____	Is easily discouraged	_____
_____	Is preoccupied with past	_____
_____	Is defensive	_____
_____	Is driven by performance	_____
_____	Talks negatively of self	_____
_____	Seeks identity through position	_____
_____	Lacks decisiveness	_____
_____	Is critical of others	_____
_____	Tends to question self	_____
_____	Compares self with others	_____
_____	Fears failure	_____
_____	Tends to believe the worst about a situation	_____
_____	Can be paralyzed by own inadequacies	_____
_____	Seeks identity through accumulation of wealth	_____
_____	Has difficulty establishing meaningful relationships	_____
_____	Hides weaknesses	_____
_____	Attempts to control others to make self look good	_____
_____	Is generally satisfied with self	_____
_____	Seeks identity through association with significant others	_____
_____	Is self-conscious	_____
_____	Has negative feelings about self	_____
_____	Has unreal expectations of self	_____
_____	Worries about what others think	_____
_____	Needs continual approval	_____
_____	Is insecure around others	_____
_____	Has difficulty opening up	_____
_____	Takes things personally	_____

B. Compare and discuss your list with your mate's list.
C. Which one or two areas tend to be major struggling points for your mate? For you?
D. Write down what your mate recommends that you do to help him in his major problem area(s).

— 4 —
Nine Laws That Liberate

WHEN FBI AGENTS are trained to spot counterfeit currency, they do not spend all their time looking at counterfeits. Instead, hours are spent carefully scrutinizing authentic $1, $5, $10, $20, $50 and $100 bills. Their training is aimed at making them so alert to what genuine currency looks like, that the imitation is easily recognizable.

Similarly, your mate needs your help in becoming *alert* to God's truth about himself. As that truth takes up residence in his life, he will begin to spot lies, counterfeit thoughts, and the bogus feelings that deny the truth. These inaccurate assessments will be exposed quickly as the forgeries they are.

Truth: A New Standard of Comparison

For security to emerge in your mate, he needs a new standard of comparison that accurately and authoritatively measures his worth and value. The truth of the Bible is just that standard. As established by God, truth is an eternal yardstick of value and worth. It does not waver with changes in society.

The concept of truth can engender all sorts of negative responses, among them "boring," "dry," "restrictive," "philosophical," and "only for deep thinkers." Yet, truth is the only standard by which all people can measure themselves accurately and confidently. It is the foundation upon which you will place the building blocks of self-esteem that follow. Without the foundation of truth, all your efforts toward building your mate will crumble as you and your mate inevitably fail each other. There is no other lasting, permanent criterion by which to know whether a person has succeeded or failed.

Truth Is Powerful

The truth of God's Word promises action — sometimes action that brings pain. "For the word of God is living and active and sharper than any two-edged sword, and piercing as far as the division of soul and spirit, of both joints and marrow, and able to judge the thoughts and intentions of the heart."[1]

Do you want to help slay your mate's unattainable phantom? Do you want to see his erroneous thoughts about himself whittled down and done away with? If so, the truth contained in Scripture is the sharp sword you need.

Truth Demands a Response

One foggy night, the captain of a large ship saw what appeared to be another ship's lights approaching in the distance. This other ship was on a course that would mean a head-on crash. Quickly the captain signaled to the approaching ship, "Please change your course 10 degrees west." The reply came blinking back through the thick fog, "You change your course 10 degrees east." Indignantly the captain pulled rank and shot a message back to the other ship, "I'm a sea captain with thirty-five years of experience. You change your course 10 degrees west!" Without hesitation the signal flashed back, "I'm a seaman fourth class. You change your course 10 degrees east!" Enraged and incensèd, the captain realized that within minutes they would crash head on so he blazed his final warning back to the fast-approaching ship: "I'm a 50,000-ton freighter. *You* change *your* course 10 degrees west!" The simple message winked back, "I'm a lighthouse. *You* change . . ."

Like the sea captain, we may need to change course when confronted with the truth. What we think is true, the phantom, may not be true at all. You or your mate may require more than a minor 10-degree alteration — you may need to change course 180 degrees. You may conclude you are going in the wrong direction altogether and handling problems in the wrong way or with the wrong attitude.

Without knowing the truths that follow, you may lose heart in seeking to build up your mate. Recognizing these truths is essential for any married partners who wish to help each other construct a positive self-image.

NINE LAWS THAT LIBERATE

Jesus said, "you shall know the truth, and the truth shall make you free."[2] Perhaps your mate is in bondage to a poor self-esteem because he has chosen (either willfully or out of a lack of knowledge) not to believe the truth.

We want to share nine truths, or laws, that will begin to liberate you and your mate as you build into one another's lives and strengthen each other's self-image. Like water saturating a sponge, these truths should permeate your relationship with your mate. Understanding and applying these laws is a prerequisite for using the ten building blocks that will follow.

 The Law of Giving

Jesus said, "Give, and it will be given to you; good measure, pressed down, shaken together, running over, they will pour into your lap. For whatever measure you deal out to others, it will be dealt to you in return."[3] The Law of Giving applies to many areas of life, but is relevant especially to our self-esteem.

Yet, a prevalent philosophy says, "You can give away only what you have." The world whispers, "Wait until your own needs are met; then you will be strong enough to reach out to others. Then you will be able to 'really' give."

Is that what Jesus meant when He said "give"? Did He put qualifiers on this command to excuse the "have nots"? We think not. Why? Perhaps Jesus knew we all would fall into the category of "have nots" to one degree or another. Then there would be no one to give and a world full of people waiting to receive.

Christianity is full of apparent paradoxes, including one that Jesus teaches us: If we give, we will receive. Somehow a transfer takes place so that when we give we are not depleted but enriched, even if we do not see it or feel it at the moment.

After hearing some of the material in this book, one woman saw this law illustrated. She wrote, "I have realized that in giving of myself, I am actually getting in return a spouse who feels good about himself, which then makes me feel good about myself."

Perhaps you get tired of giving. You may be thinking, "You don't know my mate. I don't want to give this time." You may even feel, "I don't care what the Bible says!" We understand. But when truth is not ruling, feelings are. Acting on negative feelings will not build your mate's self-image or your marriage — it will only tear down what you've already built.

Are you a giver? Remember, giving is one of the prerequisites of a great marriage. Even if you feel you've given and given and given for years, please don't give up. Your mate needs you more than you realize. Keep on giving. God sees, and He will reward you. As Paul admonished, "Let us not lose heart in doing good, for in due time we shall reap if we do not grow weary."[4]

F. B. Meyer has said, "He is the richest man in the esteem of the world who has gotten most. He is the richest man in the esteem of heaven who has given most." Where do you want to be the richest?

The Law of Understanding

A story from *Hans Brinker,* a classic in children's literature and set in nineteenth-century Holland, illustrates the Law of Understanding. It's the story of a band of young teen-age boys who took off on a grand holiday adventure. They left their small home town to skate across Holland's frozen canals and spend a few days sightseeing in the magnificent city of Amsterdam. On their way, the five young men stopped at a small inn to spend the night. After they were refreshed with a hot supper, the boys unwisely emptied their purse on the table in the public dining room and counted their money. After planning the next day's route, they went upstairs to bed.

> In the middle of the night, the leader of the boys, Peter, woke to the faint sound of someone sliding across the floor. After a scuffle, the boys bravely apprehended a would-be burglar. The prisoner was taken away by two officers and the boys and the inn's landlord were asked to appear in court the next morning.
>
> The dialogue in the courtroom was understandably heated. "The scoundrel!" said Carl [one of the boys], savagely . . ."He ought to be sent to jail at once. If I had been in your place, Peter, I certainly should have killed him outright!"
>
> "He was fortunate, then, falling into gentler hands," was Peter's quiet reply. "It appears he has been arrested before . . . this time he was armed with a knife, too, and that makes it worse for him, poor fellow."
>
> "Poor fellow!" mimicked Carl. "One would think he was your brother!"
>
> "So he is my brother, and yours too, Carl Schummel, for that matter," answered Peter. "We cannot say what we might have become under other circumstances. We have been bolstered up from evil, since the hour we were born. A happy home and good parents might have made that man a fine fellow instead of what he is."[5]

Peter's response was a rare exhibit of what the Bible refers to as understanding. Closely akin to wisdom and knowledge, understanding is defined in Noah Webster's 1828 dictionary as "the faculty of the human mind by which it . . . *comprehends*

the ideas which others express and intend to communicate"
(italics added).

Understanding, then, is not just a transference of information, but an empathy for the other person based on what was shared or communicated. In our marriage, we have found that understanding is essential in building each other's self-image. We are continually seeking to comprehend the context of each other's lives, just as Peter did with the thief. Context helps explain our self-image, our behavior and our attitudes.

Applying this Law of Understanding will give you the right to be heard by your mate. Suggestions and attempts to build into your mate will be better received if he senses you truly understand, or at least *desire* to understand.

The next time your mate expresses a concern, ask him if he feels you understand. Practice listening with a sympathetic ear, and look beyond his response to its cause. What has occurred in your mate's life in the past to contribute to his present attitude? What pressures today may be crushing his self-esteem?

Proverbs 24:3 says, "By wisdom a house is built, and by understanding it is established." Begin reconstructing your mate's self esteem and consequently you will strengthen your marriage by giving him the gift of understanding.

3 | The Law of Perseverance

In our marriage, we tend to want instant results. We want to see change yesterday. Or at the latest, now! However, contrary to our wishes, the positive changes we have seen have occurred slowly. Many are still in process.

Just as your mate's self-esteem grew through a lifetime of experiences, so it will be conformed to the truth with time as he grows in the knowledge of God and experiences His plan for his life. Have faith and hope in Jesus Christ and His sufficiency. Believe that your mate *can* and *will* change.

Paul writes of this process, "We all, with unveiled face beholding as in a mirror the glory of the Lord, *are being transformed* into the same image" (italics added).[6]

We are being transformed, we are being changed. It's not instant; it's a process of *becoming*. The Law of Perseverance warns us not to look for an immediate change. An oak tree may take as many as fifty to seventy-five years to become mature. Straw only takes three months. Which kind of growth and maturity do you want in your mate?

Charles H. Spurgeon has a word for you as you attempt to build your mate's self-image. He said, "By perseverance, the snail reached the ark." Hang in there. Perseverance will bring reward for you, just as it did for the snail.

 ## The Law of Sowing and Reaping

Picture your life, your mate's life, and your marriage when you are in your sixties or seventies. What do you envision? A vital, contagious relationship between two people who have climbed mountains together? Do you look with admiration at the one who you can proudly say has grown stronger through the gale-force winds of your lifetime? Or do you hear only the ticking of the clock and the repetitive squeaking of a rocking chair, and imagine an occasional glance into the eyes of your partner, who has become a distant stranger? A stranger who has never been free to share himself, because he was shackled by a poor self-image?

The Scriptures say, "Do not be deceived, God is not mocked; for whatever a man sows, this he will also reap."[7] What are you sowing in your mate and marriage? Are you sowing the seeds of time, creativity, encouragement and understanding? Or are you sowing weed seeds of impatience, anger, pretense, selfishness, disregard or neglect?

If at fifty or sixty or seventy you expect to enjoy the benefits of a mate who is positive about himself and about life, and a marriage that is alive and rich, then you must aggressively sow positive seed in your mate's life. A future harvest demands faithful planting and continuing cultivation today.

The Law of Teachability

The Bible repeatedly teaches that growth cannot occur without a teachable heart. We believe a teachable spirit is one of the most important components in any marriage relationship, and thus in the building of your mate's self-esteem.

By teachable spirit, we mean a progressively growing desire to learn. It requires the ability to admit fault and to ask forgiveness of one another. Ultimately it means a willingness to do what is right, what God wants, regardless of the personal sacrifice or cost.

We've found it is imperative in our relationships, with God and each other, to always retain our ability to say, "I have not arrived," "I have more to learn," "Please help me develop and mature in this area." Likewise, we encourage you to ask God regularly to give you and your mate teachable hearts that are willing to do all He has commanded.

Perhaps your mate is not teachable. Begin to pray now that he will hunger and thirst for progress and not be satisfied with mediocrity. Also, model a teachable heart in your own life. Teachability can be contagious. You may be the best example of growth your mate ever sees.

 The Law of Accountability

The Law of Accountability requires you to submit your life to another person's judgment and authority to help you live the Christian life. Paul wrote of this accountability in Ephesians 5:21: "And be subject to one another in the fear of Christ."

Submitting your life to another involves risk and fear. Yet with risk comes the hope of being known and accepted. And with acceptance comes an increase in trust and protection.

Accountability in marriage says, "I need you. You're important to me and I need you to be my partner. I want to share my life with you, because you are a *trusted friend*."

This accountability establishes a partnership of mutual protection for you and your mate. When you become accountable to your mate, you let him into the interior of your life. You may reveal a weakness for which you need advice, a temptation that is plaguing you, or a problem that you need your mate's help in solving.

Accountability works like an umbrella — it protects. Because Dennis is accountable to Barbara for his schedule, she feels a part of Dennis's life. And because Barbara is accountable to Dennis for the many objectives she tends to set, he feels trusted and a significant part of her life. God's design for marriage includes a partnership of accountability for the purposes of growth, protection, and the building of trust. And trust is non-negotiable if you are to build your mate's self-esteem.

Make your life accountable to your mate in an area in which you need his strength. As a result, watch him beam with excitement. He'll think, "My mate really does trust me!"

 ## The Law of Risk

Building your mate's self-image and ultimately your marriage necessitates taking chances. Removing your mask and letting the other person know you demands vulnerability. It is tempting to retreat from this challenge into the safety of the known and predictable. But remember, taking risks can be rewarding as you gain a stronger marriage. So be risky. Let your mate into your life and encourage him to do the same.

You can help your mate to be courageous and vulnerable by honoring his attempts to communicate. Listen and be patient. He is risking your rejection, which may be one of his most controlling fears. Like rappelling off of a ten-thousand-foot peak in the Rockies, he is dropping into the unknown, the unexplored, the untried. Encourage his attempts. And reward his efforts with approval and affirmation.

The Law of God-Given Worth

Helen Keller said, "So much has been given to me, I have no time to ponder over that which has been denied."

This blind and deaf woman was able to look beyond limiting circumstances and conditions to see that which couldn't be taken away. She realized she had been given worth and value by God. Fashioned in His image, she understood she was the pinnacle of God's creation. And she knew that, as Psalm 8:5 tells us, she was crowned with "glory and majesty."

Your mate also has worth. First, God has given him *assigned worth*. He gave value to all people as His creation and to Christians as His children.

Just as John F. Kennedy was born into the Kennedy family and thus received assigned worth, those who are born again into God's family (through faith in Christ) have assigned worth. Kennedy did nothing to deserve that prestige and position in society, just as we do not deserve our position. It is a free gift — part of our birthright — when we trust in Christ for the forgiveness of our sins.

Another illustration of assigned worth is the story of a young man kidnapped from his home in Africa and taken to America on a slave ship. After months of experiencing rotten food, disease, the stench of human wastes, and seeing the death of many around him, the young man was placed on a platform to be sold. This proud black man stood boldly with his chest out, his chin up, and his eyes fixed straight ahead.

The crowd stirred as they quickly noticed that this man was different. But why? The slave trader explained, "This boy is the son of a king in Africa and he can't forget it!"

Help your mate remember he is a child of the King. Remind him of the benefits that are his by virtue of the new birth (such as those delineated in Ephesians 1:3-14).

God also has given your mate worth by giving him the ability and responsibility to attain or achieve it. *Attained worth* is the God-given satisfaction of accomplishing a task, being obedient, or faithfully using one's talents and spiritual gifts. Although achieved by man, these accomplishments are possible only because God gave both the ability and the opportunity to make it happen.

Lee Iacocca illustrates attained worth. Born the son of an Italian immigrant, Iacocca worked his way up the corporate ladder to second in command at Ford Motor Company. After being fired by Henry Ford, Iacocca went to work for Chrysler as the chief executive officer. Chrysler's complete turnaround from bankruptcy has made Iacocca an American folk hero. He has attained a (temporary) worth and value in the *world's* eyes that few could ever hope to gain.

A Christian who obeys God and is faithful to follow Him throughout his lifetime has an even greater opportunity for attained worth. While Iacocca's human fame will last only a lifetime, your mate can gain heaven's applause and "lay up treasures" that will last through eternity by being obedient to Christ's commands.

But that's not all. God also gives the satisfaction of responsibilities well carried out on earth. He will grant your mate the privilege of experiencing accomplishment now. The result is attained value.

Buttress your mate's attained worth by reminding him of his faithfulness, his successes and his contributions, whether they be public or private. Occasionally, everyone loses sight of his personal value and needs to be reminded of past accomplishments. On the other hand, the pleasure of achievement can become one's sole measure of worth. Help your mate maintain a balance between attained worth and assigned worth. This balance will aid his being content and hinder his being driven.

 The Law of Divine Sufficiency

This book contains many principles and truths from the Bible. But these valuable principles will be only stale dogma and doctrine to you unless the person of Jesus Christ is at the center of your life. As A. W. Tozer states, "The most important thing about you is what you think about God."

To build your mate's self-esteem, Jesus Christ must be *your* sufficiency. Paul writes, "Not that we are adequate in ourselves to consider anything as coming from ourselves, but our adequacy is from God."[8]

The task of building your mate's self-image is not small, nor is it accomplished quickly. Feelings of inadequacy and hopelessness can rise suddenly and envelop you like a thick fog. During these times, the truth may seem painfully distant and even impractical, yet you can keep from being overwhelmed by focusing on the sufficiency of Christ. He is alive today, and He stands ready to guide you along the way.

Paul speaks of this sufficiency as he boasts of the person of Christ being alive and at work in him. "And He has said to me, 'My grace is sufficient for you, for power is perfected in weakness.' Most gladly, therefore, I will rather boast about my weaknesses, that the power of Christ may dwell in me . . . for when I am weak, then I am strong."[9]

Your mate's self-image can become a trophy of God's grace and power. No matter how inadequate you feel to help your mate, or how poor your mate's self-image seems, God is completely able to do what appears impossible. His power is most evident when we are weakest.

Why not submit to Him today and ask him to be your sufficiency and your strength? (If you or your mate question your relationship with God and your eternal destiny, please read the appendix at the end of this book).

Slaying the Phantom With the Truth

The application of these laws can profoundly affect your mate's self-image. His phantom will be exposed in the light of the truth. No matter how deeply his experience has bruised him, your mate can begin to be healed as you faithfully apply these truths. Your perfection is not demanded; your perseverance is. Remind your mate of these truths as you work to create an environment in your home that nourishes his self-esteem with understanding, giving, patience and prayer.

Now that the foundation is laid, the following chapters explain ten practical building blocks that will change your mate's self-esteem.

THE BUILDING BLOCKS OF SELF-ESTEEM

1. Accepting Unconditionally

Total acceptance is the most important foundation in building your mate's self-esteem. Without it, your marriage rests on the shifting sand of emotions.

2. Putting the Past in Perspective

Contribute a positive, hopeful perspective to your mate's imperfect past.

3. Planting Positive Words

Your words have the power to contaminate a positive self-image or to heal the spreading malignancy of a negative one.

4. Constructing in Difficult Times

Weather the storms of life by turning toward one another and building into each other rather than rejecting each other.

5. Giving the Freedom to Fail

Release your mate from the prison of performance with the golden key labeled "the freedom to fail."

6. Pleasing Your Mate

By focusing on pleasing your mate, you communicate that he is valued, cherished and loved.

7. Doing What Is Right

Your genuine applause for right choices will motivate your mate toward an obedient lifestyle.

8. Helping Your Mate Develop Friends

By encouraging your mate to develop close friendships, you enable others to affirm his value and significance.

9. Keeping Life Manageable

Completing the construction of your mate's self-image requires making tough decisions, knowing your values, thinking prayerfully, and keeping life simple.

10. Discovering Dignity Through Destiny

True significance is found as we invest in a cause that will outlive us.

ESTEEM BUILDER PROJECT
(Use a sheet of paper if necessary.)

The following is a list of the nine laws that liberate. Place a star next to the two or three laws you feel you need to apply to your marriage. (Don't choose so many that you feel overwhelmed!) Encourage your mate to select a couple of laws to apply also.

1. The Law of Giving
2. The Law of Understanding
3. The Law of Perseverance
4. The Law of Sowing and Reaping
5. The Law of Teachability
6. The Law of Accountability
7. The Law of Risk
8. The Law of God-Given Worth
9. The Law of Divine Sufficiency

Since all of these are attitudes and perspectives, now think of concrete ways you can demonstrate these attitudes toward your mate.

Accepting Unconditionally

Total acceptance is the most important foundation in building your mate's self-esteem. Without it, your marriage rests on the shifting sand of emotions.

— 5 —

Dealing With the Good, the Bad and the Otherwise in Your Mate

---

- Adam and Eve on Stage
- "Should We Keep Her?"
- God Speaks About Marriage — Leaving, Cleaving, and Becoming One Flesh
- The Great Mistake and What Happened Afterward
- Creating a Garden Experience in Your Marriage
- Making Acceptance Flourish
- What About Differences?
- Living With Your Mate's Differences
- Praying for Yourself
- Talking to Your Mate
- Tutor Your Mate With His Permission
- Ignoring Differences
- Continue to Verbalize Commitment
- Accept Your Mate Unconditionally
- Esteem Builder Project

Building Block 1: Accepting Unconditionally

IN THE FAMILIAR account of God's gift of Eve to Adam, we find the basis for unconditionally accepting your mate. In scene one, Adam, though secure in his own self-esteem and knowing his worth and value, makes a discovery: He is alone. God allows Adam to feel that aloneness in order to prepare him for His plan, to be revealed in scene two.

The stage is set for scene two: the crucial introduction and first meeting. The curtain rises. The audience, heaven's angels, falls silent.

God and Eve enter the stage where Adam is already on location. God presents Eve to Adam as His perfect provision for Adam's experienced need. She is God's solution to Adam's problem. Then the high point of this scene occurs: Adam completely accepts God's gift — Eve.[1] The audience cheers. The curtain falls.

Before we yawn over the familiarity of the story, let's think for a minute about this crucial scene. What if Adam had said, "She's not what I had in mind, but there's no other choice, so I'll take her." How would Eve have felt? Would she have felt accepted? No. Adam's response was complete acceptance. There was no rejection. There were no conditions.

What about Eve? Was she just a puppet in this play? We don't think so. Eve made a choice, too. What if she had rejected Adam in any way? She had no way of knowing what kind of husband he would be to her. She couldn't check out his parents or talk to his friends.

Adam and Eve made commitments to receive and accept each other as God's gift and provision for their need on the basis of faith in God. They knew their creator. They knew He was loving and that He could be trusted.

We have had the privilege of experiencing this "acceptance by faith" with each other. In a similar way, we have received six children from the hands of God. Before our last child was born, we both had guessed it would be a boy. With all our experience we expected our intuition to be accurate, especially since we agreed this time. But on a cold, clear January evening, three hours after we arrived at the hospital, the doctor held up our new baby and said, "It's a girl!"

Suppose we immediately had held a conference — just the two of us — and the following conversation transpired:

"There must be a mistake; it was supposed to be a boy."

"She looks a little blue, don't you think?"

"You're right, and I wonder if she'll be a good baby."

"You never know."

"Well, what do you think? Should we keep her?"

"Let's vote."

Obviously, that conversation never took place. There was never a question, never a doubt. We received her and accepted her as God's gift to us without knowing anything about her. We did, however, know and trust the God who gave her to us. So we reached out and took her, and, holding her in those early moments of her life, began to build a relationship. We knew this was the child God had given to us.

Accepting your mate as God's gift is very similar. And that unconditional acceptance is based on a belief in God's ability to provide what's best. In reaching out and receiving Eve from God's hand, Adam made a commitment to her. From that commitment, Eve experienced acceptance to be who she was created to be. She felt no pressure to be anyone else.

A Word From God to the Audience

At the end of scene two, after the curtain closes, God steps out of the action to address the audience.

"For this cause a man shall leave his father and his mother, and shall cleave to his wife; and they shall become one flesh."[2]

Thus, God has given us as observers a mandate describing how two people are to become one. Here are His three steps.

Step one is to *leave*. We tend to think of leaving as a physical move, which most of us made when we married. We left our parents' homes and moved into our own home.

But God has much more in mind. The old adage of "cutting the apron strings" is closer to the truth than a move with Mayflower Van Lines. To leave means "to sever dependence upon." It means to cut the lines of emotional and financial support from your parents and to tie those lines into your mate.

Yet for many, the apron strings are not cut; they are only lengthened. It's called "Operation Rescue" — with "good old" mom and dad coming to rescue their distressed child! Your mate may feel he has to compete with the in-laws for your dependence and loyalty. To sever does not mean to terminate the relationship, but it does mean that your dependence and allegiance is first and foremost to your mate. Your mate is to demonstrate that same "severing" and "dependence" for you.

In step two, God commands us to *cleave* to one another. To cleave means "to form a permanent bond, to make a commitment." It's similar to the process of combining two different metals to make a new metal, an alloy. The process can't be reversed. Likewise, God's intent for marriage is an irreversible commitment — a permanent commitment with no escape clauses.

This explicit bonding commitment is essential. It is only as you absolutely and resolutely commit yourself permanently to your mate that you give him the freedom to grow in his self-esteem.

The third step, the result of leaving and cleaving, is to *become one flesh.* It begins on the wedding night with physical intercourse and continues throughout the years of marriage. Becoming one, becoming that new alloy, is a process. Oneness takes time, but it can't happen without the leaving and the commitment of cleaving.

The Fatal Choice

As the play continues on stage, we watch Adam and Eve enjoying a perfect relationship through accepting one another. But as their story develops, we observe in scene three the fatal encounter with the serpent, Satan (Genesis 3:1-5). Two choices to disobey God were made and all of history was forever marred.

Notice the first result of their sin: Adam said to God, "I was *afraid* because I was naked; so I hid myself" (Genesis 3:10).

Fear was the first result of sin. Adam and Eve had never felt fear before, but that feeling compelled them to do something foreign. They covered themselves from each other. They hid behind fig leaves. Then they hid again, from God. How foolish they were to hide from God, but they felt they had to. Sin and fear were now their masters.

Adam and Eve once knew perfect acceptance in their relationship with each other and with God. Now they lived only with the memory of it and with their new companion: fear. The fear of rejection now plagued their fellowship with God and with each other.

Today we know the fear, but have no idea what that perfect acceptance was like. Yet God, in His grace, has given us as husbands and wives the opportunity to taste some of the freedom that Adam and Eve knew in their pre-fall days: complete, untainted acceptance.

Creating a Garden Experience in Your Marriage

How do you establish this kind of relationship in marriage? First, as Adam and Eve did, receive your mate as God's gift to you. Don't focus on the imperfections or the differences. focus on the giver, the one who is sovereign, the one who doesn't make mistakes. Sincerely thank God for your mate, just as Adam and Eve did, by faith.

Second, make a commitment to one another. Tell your mate that you accept him as God's gift. Acknowledge that truth verbally to each other. Say, "I accept you as God's gift to me. I trust Him in His choice of you for me." That in itself will do a lot to build worth in your mate.

Once you've completed the leaving and cleaving — when you've committed to accept one another completely — then and only then can you begin to work constructively on step three: becoming one. Becoming one is far more than the physical act of marriage. It's the blending of two individuals into one unit, two distinct personalities yet inseparably linked. Building that oneness requires a solid and firm foundation of acceptance, which also is critical to a secure marriage and a secure self-image in your mate.

Making Acceptance Flourish

The most important step in building your mate's self-image and self-worth is to accept him unconditionally. This is not a resigned, defeated acceptance, but an acceptance that embraces your mate with expectancy and excitement. That's how Adam received Eve. He accepted her based on his knowledge of God. Adam had a friendship with God and since he knew he could trust God as his provider, he accepted His gift.

Your mate needs the same kind of acceptance. If your acceptance is not complete, the gaps in your commitment will be filled by rejection — the opposite of acceptance. Your mate's companions will be fear and insecurity, rather than the security of being completely, unconditionally accepted. He may go through a personality change and become inhibited and unresponsive. He may feel he has to perform or put on a front to merit your conditional acceptance.

When you unconditionally accept your mate, though, you give him the freedom to be on the outside who he really is on the inside. Your acceptance communicates love, value and need, and gives him self-confidence and a reprieve from having to "fake it" in the world. With you, he can remove the masks, be real and begin to see the fear of rejection and failure melt away.

Perhaps you made your foundational commitment with relative ease and set out to do right, but along the way you've stopped accepting your mate. You've found yourself subtly trying to change him. When you concentrate on changing your mate, you focus on his negative qualities (from your perspective) rather than his positive ones. You put yourself in an authority position in your mate's life. You actually try to take God's place and orchestrate change. Your mate then becomes defensive and suddenly it's no longer a partnership, but a civil war.

If this is your situation, it is time to renew your commitment and to remember that only God can change lives. He may change those qualities in your mate, or He may not. Either way, your unconditional acceptance is vital to your marriage and to your mate's self-esteem.

What About Differences?

Like tiny black gnats at a summer picnic, differences can buzz in your ears, threatening to rob your relationship of its peaceful, accepting love. As Sam Levenson said, "Love at first sight is easy to understand; it's when two people have been looking at each other for a lifetime that it becomes a miracle!" Someone else has said, "Love is blind, but marriage is an eye-opener." As you move past the honeymoon, all those differences, those little "eye-openers," begin to affect your marriage.

Ironically, differences are those wonderful qualities that attracted you to each other when dating. He was outgoing, she was shy; he was a big spender, which made her feel special because she was a tightwad; he was a hard worker, she was impulsive and fun-loving. Opposites attract. It works like magnetism.

But when the honeymoon fades and reality sets in, those attractive uniquenesses often become aggravating differences or weaknesses. The very things that initially attracted you to your mate now repel or frustrate you.

As a result, you are faced with several decisions. First and foremost, you must ask yourself, "Will I continue to accept my mate in this particular area of difference, or will I withdraw a portion of my acceptance, thereby driving a sliver of rejection between us?" You cannot ignore the question, because the differences won't go away. If you can't accept that quality, you are rejecting (silently or verbally) your mate, and his self-image will suffer. Your only two options are to accept him or reject him.

LIVING WITH YOUR MATE'S DIFFERENCES

If you choose acceptance, then another question arises:

"How do I live with this difference?" The answer is multiple choice, with more than one, or possibly all, of the choices being correct in any given situation.

1. Pray for yourself.

Begin by praying for yourself. Ask God to make you content with your mate as he is. Pray, too, that God will show you the positive side of your mate's apparently negative quality.

In our relationship, Dennis and I (Barbara) are extreme opposites on the impulsive/disciplined scale. When we were first married his impulsiveness tended to drive my disciplined nature crazy. I *felt* that we had no order, no schedule, no budget, no regular devotions.

I remember praying diligently for God to change all these things I didn't like. Then I realized what really needed to be changed was my attitude. God did change my perspective and in time I began to see how much I needed Dennis's impulsiveness to balance my discipline.

Ask God to examine your attitudes and your motives, and to give you a greater capacity to understand and accept your mate's differences. This step may be necessary before God can use you to elevate your mate's self-image.

2. Talk about it with your mate.

Ask for the privilege of being heard. Tell him you are not rejecting him in this area of difference and that you remain committed. Assure him that he is loved no matter what. One thing we have learned in our marriage is that at some moments we are teachable and at others learning is unlikely. Unless it is obvious, we determine whether the time is opportune by asking.

If you find it is not the time to talk, leave the subject alone. Don't try to force an issue with which your mate is not emotionally ready to deal.

You also may discover that the territory you are about to encroach upon is marked "NO TRESPASSING." It may be off limits at this point in his life. If so, be satisfied with exploring small bits of land at a time. Do not hope to cover the whole country in one evening. Go slowly.

If your mate is willing to talk about the difference that is bothering you, share your feelings without accusing him and pointing the finger of blame. Don't be critical. Let him know you are not perfect and that you understand him, or want to understand him, in this area. Realize, too, that we all have weaknesses or tendencies that we will never completely conquer. Because of our fallen nature, perfection will never be ours until we reach heaven.

If your mate considers the difference a weakness, ask if you can help. Then, at the end of your discussion, remind your mate again of your commitment and acceptance. We call this the bookend principle. Just as bookends are used to prop up books that contain truth, so your reminders of complete acceptance at both ends of the discussion will support the truth of what you have said. And it makes the truth *easier* to hear.

3. Tutor your mate with his permission.

As a couple, we continue to assist one another with many areas, such as punctuality, patience with children, planning, feelings of discouragement and depression, one partner's tendency to be impulsive and the other's tendency to be too controlled. We have found that the many opposites that attracted us when we dated, which became repellents after we married, are the very things that have balanced us. Our differences have made us more effective as a couple than we ever could have been alone.

One area in which I (Barbara) have assisted Dennis is in his public speaking. Early in our marriage, I noticed he was making some obvious grammatical errors as he spoke. I felt free to offer help because, on more than one occasion, I had told him honestly that he communicated well.

So, one evening after he had spoken, I asked Dennis if I could make a suggestion that might make him more effective as a speaker. He said, "Yes." Although my critique was a little threatening, he confessed he didn't do well in English in school, and he said he welcomed my suggestions.

Several years later, on the way home from another speaking opportunity, Dennis told me, "I still want you to help me with my speaking, but I'd like you to wait a little while before you tell me the cold, hard truth."

I realized my technique of helping him needed refining. I had become truthful too quickly. My "help" became a discouragement because it wasn't seasoned with enough praise or separated far enough from the actual event. Had I not modified my recommendations, I would have crossed the fine line separating acceptance from rejection.

If your mate has granted you permission to help, ask God for wisdom in how to help. Offer your assistance in such a way that your mate experiences your acceptance and in no way senses rejection.

4. Ignore them.

Some of the differences that annoy you may not be weaknesses in your mate. Commit those differences to the Lord in prayer, asking Him to give you peace and contentment to live with them, even if your mate never changes. It is important to accept him "as is," without pressure to change. Choose to ignore the differences that are off limits and seemingly beyond change, and rejoice over the many benefits you enjoy because of your partner's strengths and your relationship together.

Continue to Verbalize Commitment

Several years ago, God gave us the wonderful privilege of helping a couple to resurrect a marriage that seemed beyond hope. The changes were dramatic. The commitments to Christ and to each other were real, and they grew steadily in their relationship.

But one day, the wife came in discouraged about their marriage. They had reached an area of difference they couldn't resolve. Each time they argued about this, the husband threatened to leave, which was a tactic from the past. Unwittingly, he was saturating their relationship with the fear that maybe he would leave.

A threat of leaving puts cracks in the commitment and tears down the security of total acceptance. One of the Ten Commandments of Marriage should be, "Never threaten to leave." It does nothing but cause fear to increase. Threats rarely cause a person to change. They only imply rejection.

Rather than threaten to leave, we should creatively and continually express our commitment and acceptance. God gave us an example to follow. He didn't just say once that He loved us; He told us and showed us in many ways. Then He sent His Son to demonstrate it, and He gave us His Word to read over and over so we wouldn't forget it. He continues to show us His love today through His Holy Spirit.

Our mates need to hear those words of commitment and acceptance from us not just once, but many, many times. Tell your mate often of your commitment to him. Tell him you accept him just as he is.

Each time a difficulty arises in your relationship, whether it is a misunderstanding, a difference, or a clash of the wills, remind your mate (even in the heat of a battle if necessary) that you are loyal to him. Assure him that your commitment will not change because of this particular situation. Tell him you accept him just as he is. Those infusions of truth will become the reinforcements needed to work through the difficulties in your marriage. Total acceptance motivates you both to persevere in the relationship.

Also tell your mate occasionally that you'd choose to marry him again. It gives him value and approval and builds his self-esteem. It reminds him of the truth that he is accepted, and that brings deep satisfaction.

Throughout our years of marriage, we continue to see potential threats surface unexpectedly. Attitudes, ideas, fears, temptations and old memories all arise to threaten our mutual acceptance. We may wonder, *What would he think if he knew this thought?* or *What would she think if she knew how I felt?*

Experiencing acceptance is a process. As one tests the water temperature of a swimming pool before diving in, so marriage partners test each other before revealing themselves. The revelation is sometimes risky, but necessary. Learn when to talk, what to say, how much to say and what words to use. Communicate with wisdom.

Accept Your Mate Unconditionally

Why is unconditional acceptance so important? Because if you accept only in part, you can love only in part. And if you love in part, your mate's self-esteem will never be complete. That area of rejection will keep your mate from becoming all he was meant to be.

Remember, "Perfect love casts out fear."[3] If your love does not fill your mate's life completely, you leave room for fear to take up residence. And fear, as we have seen, is central in an insecure self-image. Following Adam and Eve's example, couples still hide from one another for fear of being known and, thus, rejected. When our self-esteem is low, we protect ourselves fiercely from exposure.

But the hope for marriage is that we can find the security to dare to be real. That security can come only from complete acceptance by another. It gives us confidence that says, "The whole world may reject me, but my mate won't." That is security.

Remember that complete unconditional acceptance will begin to set your mate free from self-doubt, from the fear of failure, and from an incorrect self-image — free to be his best. It will build self-confidence and hope. Your faith and belief in him will help him see himself as God does — worthy and valuable.

A familiar saying states, "He who knows you best, loves you most." As you know and accept your mate, your love — as well as his self-image — will grow.

ESTEEM BUILDER PROJECT

(Use a sheet of paper if necessary.)

1. Are there any cracks in your acceptance of your mate (areas of his life where you don't accept him)? If so, what do you need to do to grant total acceptance?
2. Are there differences or weaknesses in your mate that continually bother you? List them and thank God for them.
3. Will you accept your mate from God as His provision for you? Write out a commitment and contract with God to accept your mate fully.
4. How can you pray positively for your mate? List at least three qualities to ask God to develop in his life.

Putting the Past in Perspective

Contribute a positive, hopeful perspective to your mate's imperfect past.

— 6 —
Helping Your Mate Clean Out the Attic of the Past

- The "Thing" in Dennis's Attic
- The Past and Your Mate's Self-Esteem
- The Dark Corner of Parents
- One Woman's Story
- Warning Signals From His Home Life
- A Reprieve for Parents
- Getting Out of the Corner — Six Steps
- The Dark Corner of Peers
- Poisonous Tongues
- Getting Out of the Dark Corner of Peer Pressure
- Skeletons in the Corner
- Cleaning Up the Past's Dark Corner — Five Steps
- Be on Guard Against Unseen Forces
- Esteem Builder Project

Building Block 2: Putting the Past in Perspective

AS A FIVE-YEAR-OLD boy growing up in a small, white two-story frame home, I (Dennis) was terrified of one place: the attic. An eerie stillness enveloped me as I ventured into this windowless, hot, creepy room. The scent of moth balls perfumed the air. The attic was laced with invisible threads of spider webs which feebly attempted to capture me if I got too near. Mysterious shapes, covered by sheets and blankets, crouched in corners, casting suspicious shadows on the plank floor. A solitary light bulb swung from the ceiling, but invariably it was burned out.

I just knew that attic contained more than discarded junk. Something was living up there, something that would mercilessly defend its territory against weaker, pint-sized trespassers. I

83

never saw this creature, but I knew it was there. And I feared that I would get locked in that dark, dusty, despicable garret, alone with the "thing."

Everyone has an attic in which the past is stored. It's a place where emotionally-charged relics still live under sheets and in boxes, tucked into the corners of our minds. Those memories, of when we failed others and when others failed us, haunt and accuse. They also significantly contribute to the makeup of our own and our mates' self-images.

As a child, I feared going into the attic alone, but with a companion, I became downright courageous. That dark, scary spot in my home became little more than just another room. Sure, my heart still quickened a bit as I opened the door, but somehow fear was put to flight with a trusted friend beside me.

Likewise, your mate may be extremely fearful of visiting his attic of the past alone. But his confidence will grow if you go with him and uncover together the musty relics that assault his self-image. Your mate needs your help in sorting out the genuine antiques — the good esteem-building memories — from the counterfeit junk produced by the phantom and past negative experiences.

The Past and Your Mate's Self-Esteem

It has been said that the person whose problems are all behind him is probably a school bus driver. Seriously, no one can say he is totally free from his past. Problems we encountered as children most likely still confront us as adults. Things we were told we couldn't do right as a child probably have become the things we can't do right as an adult.

Today, many Christians are imprisoned by the attics of their past and need to break out. Your mate may be one of them. To help release him we must first help him determine what fills his attic and what things from the past affect his self-esteem.

THE DARK CORNER OF PARENTS' MISTAKES

Probably no human relationship evokes more emotional response, good and bad, than one's relationship with his parents. Unquestionably your mate's parents were two of the most influential people in developing his self-esteem. Their attitudes, feelings and actions were recorded in your mate as a young child. They formed the basis for his self-image.

Whether your mate was praised and encouraged continually or relentlessly criticized will largely determine how he feels about himself today. Your husband's identity as a man, or your wife's confidence as a woman, came from the relationship your mate had with his or her role model. The stability or instability of your mate's parents' marriage sent out emotional messages of security or insecurity.

Pleasing the most important people in our lives should give us a feeling of worth and value. Yet a child needs to feel valued not just for his performance and his accomplishments, but for who he is. Parents who withhold this unconditional acceptance create an adult who must perform to be valuable. He looks to others for the missing approval.

One Woman's Story

Sue and Rich dated and fell in love during college. Soon they were engaged, and finally, married. Although Sue had shared many things openly as they dated, Rich had no idea how the lack of her father's unconditional approval had shaped her self-image and influenced her life.

When Sue was six years old, her militaristic father inspected her bedroom every Friday evening. In preparation, she would balance one chair on another to dust the tops of the window and door facings, which her father routinely examined. Any other work she was required to do was scrutinized just as intently. On one occasion, she was grounded for two weeks for missing two sprigs of crabgrass when she weeded the lawn. When Sue was eleven, she had to carry two cases of Coca-Cola down the basement stairs. She barely could manage to pick them up, but she did. Halfway down, she tripped and fell head over heels to the concrete floor. She was lying in the midst of broken glass and spilled Coke when her father jerked her up and, without inquiring about her well-being, said, "You dummy, I told you not to drop them!"

Not surprisingly, Sue had an impoverished self-image. At times, during her marriage, her insecurity surfaced in the form of emotional withdrawal or of giving her husband the silent treatment. Rich was often caught off guard, but he encouraged her to share her feelings. He rarely said, "You shouldn't feel that way." Instead, he acknowledged her emotions as true feelings, though not always the truth. He remained committed to helping her resolve, and not repress, her feelings about her parents. As a result, her self-esteem has improved, and she has a positive perspective of those things she once considered negative.

Another woman never received her mother's approval. She tells how she feels as an adult today: "Just once I'd like to hear my mother compliment me on something. I'd be elated if she would say something nice about the wife and mother I am. But there's seldom a kind word." She went on, "I'm

---

WARNING SIGNALS FROM A PERSON'S HOME LIFE

The following series of warning signals could indicate your mate's self-image was adversely affected by his relationship with his parents.

Characteristics of home life:
- A home where mistakes weren't tolerated.
- A home where the father was distant, aloof and authoritative.
- A home where to admit need was to be weak.
- A home where either father or mother was gone a lot.
- A home where worth was tied to performance.

Characteristics of parents:
- Parents who were so self-sufficient they never admitted their need of anyone.
- Parents who never admitted they were wrong, nor asked forgiveness, nor ever expressed love and affection.
- Parents who didn't allow their children to be children — they expected them to behave as adults.
- A parent or parents who habitually expected too much and seldom expressed satisfaction for a job well done.

Characteristics of life now:
- A feeling that he could never please his parents even as an adult.
- An abnormal feeling of need for parental approval or a preoccupation with what Mom and Dad "think."

fifty-five years old and you'd think that what I do would be good enough. It depresses me so. I feel so low."

Your mate also may be striving for the parental approval and acceptance he missed as a child. Assisting him in dealing with his past is the pivotal point between healing a damaged self-image and leaving it needy and incomplete.

A Reprieve for Parents

Before you accuse us of being too harsh on parents and laying all the blame on them, let us assure you of three important facts.

First, everyone is born imperfect. All of us start life with the seeds of negative self-worth already planted within us because we're relatives of Adam and Eve. Nothing your mate's parents could have done would have changed this fact.

Second, no parents are perfect. No one sets out to ruin his child, but all parents make many, many mistakes in raising their children. Some do a better job of parenting than others in certain areas, but no mother or father does it perfectly. More than likely your mate's parents did the best they could.

Third, we can't blame our parents for what is our responsibility today. Although your mate's parents made errors, he is responsible for his present responses to them — not only for what they did wrong, but also what they did right.

Consequences in Your Mate's Self-Image

As a result of his parents' mistakes, your spouse may feel somewhat insecure about himself. He also may experience guilt, fear and anger toward his parents.

Does your mate feel guilty because he didn't fulfill his parents' expectations? Is he plagued by guilt over something he said or should have said, or something he wishes he'd never done?

Perhaps your spouse feels intimidated by authority figures and the implied failure they represent because he had no loving relationship with his parents. This fear of failing may dominate his life, leading him to live cautiously and never to take unnecessary risks.

Or he may be angry, full of resentment toward his parents. Your spouse may refuse to forgive them in hopes of punishing them for what he suffered as a child. Yet, holding on to bitterness and anger is more detrimental to him than to the parents he seeks to punish.

One young man revealed to us his insecurity, which he traced to his father's neglect of him as he grew up. He explained, "My father traveled a lot. He always was gone and was too busy to write or call. He completely neglected me. I never knew if he would be proud of the way I was growing up or not. Today, I still feel directionless. I'm sad for me, bitter against him, and scared about my future."

Getting Out of the Corner

Getting your mate out of this dark corner of his parents' imperfections is essential if you are to help him build a positive self-esteem. If you and your mate do not put the past behind you, then you will always be behind your past. The following are some tips for helping your mate in this area.

First, begin to work with your spouse to get the problem fully on the table. Talk about how your parents treated you and ask your mate to share his experiences. Be patient. Talking about these things can be very painful. Affirm and strengthen your mate by listening and by verbally expressing encouragement and acceptance.

Second, help your mate understand his parents. Talk together about them and put their lives in a proper perspective. Remind him that they did the best they could. They probably never read a book about parenting (unless your mate is of the Dr. Spock generation) nor had any other training.

Third, give your mate the perspective that God's grace and power is greater than his parents' mistakes. No matter how poor a person's home was, God delights in resurrecting a damaged self-image and restoring dignity to that person. Point your mate to Christ and the hope He offers by verbally drawing his attention to that truth and by expressing your confidence and belief in the greatness of God.

Fourth, help your mate determine how he will respond to his parents. He has no control over how he was treated as a child, but he does have control over how he will relate to them today. Bring his focus to what they did right by pointing out those things and how you both are the benefactors. This is important even if the parents are no longer living. Sometimes the memory of a deceased parent can be powerful, especially if the memory harbors bitterness.

Fifth, encourage your mate to forgive his parents — completely. Pray that he will choose to deal with his past constructively. Forgiveness is a choice. Perhaps, after several conversations about his parents, you could schedule a weekend getaway or an evening alone in which he could think about and deal with his feelings toward his parents. Persuade him to empty out that dark corner of his past by listing on a piece of paper everything he can think of for which he may resent them. He may need to add wrong attitudes he has held toward his parents.

You may need to talk this out first as a couple. A qualified counselor also may be necessary if you feel you cannot help your mate get on top of this emotionally-charged area and be able to forgive his parents.

Bring his attention to the fact that Paul implores us to forgive "each other, just as God in Christ also has forgiven [us]."[1] To forgive someone means to give up the right of punishment. Urge your mate to put away those punishing emotions and to replace them with an attitude of love and understanding.

Also, remind your mate of 1 John 1:9: "If we confess our sins, He is faithful and righteous to forgive us our sins and to cleanse us from all unrighteousness." Your mate may find it helpful to write this verse across his list and then to tear it up, symbolizing the forgiveness and erasing of these things from his life.

After confessing these sins to God, it may be appropriate for your mate to ask his parents' forgiveness for wrong attitudes. But he should *not* expect anything in return. Be sure your mate isn't hoping to point out how his parents were wrong or expecting them to "see the light" and ask his forgiveness also.

If your mate decides to confess to his parents, first talk together about what he should say and not say. Discourage him from accusing his parents in any way. Then, before going, pray as a couple to be sure this is God's leading, and ask God to season your mate's words with love, humility and grace. Also, ask God to prepare his parents' hearts to receive your mate's conciliatory actions.

While you can do much to encourage your spouse in this area, you can't remove the sting of his past relationship with his parents yourself. You can't make him believe what God says about His grace and His healing power. Nor can you force him to go through the process of forgiveness. It must be his choice, his belief, his decision. So, above all, pray diligently for him. Only God can give him the heart to obey.

Sixth, as a couple, aggressively begin to honor his parents. This is the initiating side of forgiveness. It not only will bring blessing to his parents, but it also will give you and your mate a sense of well-being about life, and thus a positive sense of self-worth. This is seen in one of the Ten Commandments: "Honor your father and your mother, as the LORD your God has commanded you, that your days may be prolonged, *and that it may go well* with you on the land which the LORD your God gives you" (italics added).[2]

Look for ways to help your mate bless his parents. Letters, phone calls, a care package in the dead of winter, pictures, plenty of hugs, and verbal "thank you's" for all they've done for both of you will cumulatively communicate to them love, respect and honor.

A letter that I (Dennis) received from a young woman in a graduate class I was teaching demonstrates the power of honoring parents. It illustrates the effects of a parent-child relationship and the positive results of dealing with that past as God directed and as outlined above.

> Dear Mr. Rainey,
> My father physically abused me when I was a child. He would beat me so badly that at times I didn't think I was going to live. At other times, my mom was in such fear for me that she would call the police.
> But perhaps even worse than the physical abuse was the mental abuse. Oh, how he hated me! He would cuss and scream at me every possible word you could think of and a lot you probably couldn't think of. When he was silent, the raw hate in his eyes spoke almost louder than words.
> Also while growing up, I was sexually abused by my two older brothers. If I had told anyone, they would have beaten me up, and who would I tell anyway? Finally we got caught; how thankful I was! Then someone hugged me and assured me it wouldn't happen again, right? Wrong. I was beaten again, told it was my fault and lived with dirty, obscene comments about it for months.
> During my freshman year in college, I became a Christian. My life began to change rapidly. Over the next year and a half, God took me from tremendous hate toward my father, to a dislike, to a like, until I could say I loved my father.

Then I began to find out certain things. My father was abused as a child. No one ever told me that before. His father kicked him out when he was seventeen. That must have been hard. Well, what about my mom? How come she stood by and let my father abuse us? Her first husband was an alcoholic and beat her, so she left him. Even though she worked two jobs, on many evenings there was nothing to eat for her and the three boys. That must have been hard. Then, she had to stay awake at night to guard the baby crib or else the rats would eat on the baby all night. No wonder she was scared to leave her second husband.

Does this excuse what happened to me as a child? No. Does it make it more understandable? Yes.

My father still yells and cusses at me, but you know what? Not quite so loudly. I call him on special occasions, I share my life with him and ask his advice. His response? Not so good, but that's O.K. The other day I heard he was bragging about me at work. There's hope.

This young woman came from one of the most difficult backgrounds imaginable. She suffered much. Yet she *chose* to be set free from her understandable, but nonetheless wrong, response to her father by giving forgiveness.

As you support your mate in dealing with negative attitudes toward his parents, it is imperative you realize that the choice of forgiving and honoring is his, and it most likely will take time. We are very human creatures, and at times enslaved to our emotions. Give your mate the freedom, the space, the grace and the time to work through his feelings toward his parents. In some cases, it may take months or even years for all of the hurt to be brought out in the open. Your mate needs your patient understanding, particularly in this area of his life.

THE DARK CORNER OF PEER PRESSURE

Second only to the home in influencing our lives is our relationship with peers. They were the people we tried to impress the most. And, depending on whether we were inside or outside of the "in-group," our self-image either soared or sank.

I (Dennis) will never forget how, when I was a young boy in first grade, a few friends and I began to cruelly choose who was "in" and who was "out." One of the first "outs" was Lois. She came from a very poor family and couldn't dress as well as others. She also was slow in class, which didn't help.

So Lois was quickly excluded. The "in" group rejected her as a person, slowly at first, but ruthlessly as the years passed. By the time we reached high school, she was the butt of countless jokes. When we were seniors she had such an inferiority complex that I don't recall seeing her eyes that entire year.

Some eight years later, when I read Dr. James Dobson's book on self-esteem, *Hide or Seek,* I saw my false values and my haughty, foolish evaluation of Lois. I wept when I thought about my cruelty to her. I sought forgiveness for my arrogant, childish behavior.

Peers can have poisonous tongues. William Hazlitt wrote at the turn of the nineteenth century: "A nickname is the hardest stone the devil can throw at a man." Do you know what your mate was called growing up? Do you recall some of the names others were called?

Here are a few nicknames we've come across: Dummy, Pit-i-ful Paul, Messy, Fatso, Peewee, Runt, Brick-Brain, Ornery, Grasshopper Brain, Yo-Yo, Troublemaker, Slow Learner, Bones, Motor-Mouth, Sloppy, Sleepy, Devil's Daughter, Nerd, Turkey, Lardo, Bird Legs, Space Cadet, Rebellious, Simple Sally, Buzzard-Beak, Metal-Mouth, Freckle-Face, Weirdo and Geek. All very highly motivational names!

Did your mate's peers call him a name? If so, they helped tear down his sense of worthiness. And their handiwork was done at a very crucial time in the formation of his self-worth.

Even today, your mate may be very peer dependent. He may self-conciously wonder if he's wearing "just the right things," or he may doubt his ability to relate to his spouse's peers with the right "lingo." Many adults are still influenced by the pressure to conform to the values of their peers.

Getting Out of the Dark Corner of Peer Pressure

Those haunting songs that were sung about your mate, those grinning faces he just knew were laughing at him, all echo in his mind, leaving him feeling less than acceptable. But you can help free your mate from those feelings.

Begin by deciding on your own value system. What is truly valuable and important to you both, and why? What are the values and standards by which you want to measure your lives?

If you and your mate do not have your own set of convictions (your own scales of worth and value), then you will end up using the world's. You will be peer dependent, and what the world says is valuable will be the vacillating standard by which your lives will be measured.

As a couple, study the Scriptures together. Learn what God values, such as serving people, obedience, and a supreme love for Jesus Christ. By bringing your lives into conformity with God's values, you will have a unique set of convictions that give both of you ultimate value. *Your convictions*, not those of the masses, will determine how you live and therefore how you feel about yourselves.

Also, discuss with your mate his past relationships with peers and see how they have affected his self-image. Do some scenes that play over and over in his mind, remind him of who he wasn't and what he didn't do right? Ask him to share those, and then discuss the false values that those peers were perpetuating. As a couple, compare those values with God's.

Then encourage your mate to forgive and to begin to forget. Forgiveness of peers is as important as forgiveness of parents.

Finally, invest your life in values that will last. Pour your lives into these values and teach others to do the same.

A few values that have allowed us to "break from the herd" are: the value of our family; ministering to others' spiritual needs; helping the poor and the hungry; and sharing with others the good news of Jesus Christ. These all bring ultimate value, worth and meaning to our lives.

Paul gave us a tip on our self-image when he encouraged us to break away from the world's mold and conform ourselves to God's value system. "I urge you therefore, brethren, by the mercies of God, to present your bodies a living and holy sacrifice, acceptable to God, which is your spiritual service of worship. And do not be conformed to this world, but be transformed by the renewing of your mind, that you may prove what the will of God is, that which is good and acceptable and perfect."[3]

SKELETONS IN THE CORNER

The third monster lurking in the corner of your mate's

attic comes from the past in general. It may be a mistake that accuses and condemns his worth as a person, telling him he does not merit your love and acceptance; or perhaps wrong choices, poor judgment, or some secret sin haunts him. Is he burdened by guilt over a sexual experience from his childhood or adolescence, or possibly even a willful rebellion against God in breaking one of His laws?

If your mate has been divorced, he carries a certain sense of failure and rejection from that experience. Or, if you have been divorced, your mate may fear the unknown of your past. Divorce is never easy, never painless, never simple. Its effect on your mate and your marriage cannot be ignored. This skeleton from the past must be met and reckoned with repeatedly.

Memories That Haunt

Bitter memories of past failures can vandalize your mate's self-concept. Tearing and ripping his self-portrait, these failures attack and then retreat, but they never leave. Your mate's inner beauty is smudged by the guilt attached to these scarring memories of failures, foolishness and folly.

Such guilt can be domineering. One woman confided in me (Dennis) that she and her husband of one year had not yet sexually consummated their marriage relationship. Although her husband had remained very patient, she was suffering extreme self-condemnation.

She went on to share how she had been assaulted sexually three times during her early adolescent years. She had told no one until now. She had convinced herself it was her fault and that she should bear the consequences.

But now she was frozen in guilt and fear in her relationship with her husband. She wondered, "If he knew, would he truly accept me?"

At my encouragement, she finally shared each of the traumatic experiences with her understanding husband. His acceptance of and patience with her changed her life. Slowly her fear melted, and with it, much of her self-condemnation. Her husband was instrumental in delivering her from the captivity of the past.

CLEANING UP THE PAST'S DARK CORNER

God can use you to help release your mate from the

haunting memories stored in his attic.

First, never pry about the past, but let your spouse know you are always available to listen. Each of us seems to have a morbid curiosity about the failures of others. Yet, there is no need to have the gory particulars brought into your marriage relationship. Details serve only to kindle our imaginations, causing us to replay a scene or an event. They could tempt you to condemn your mate.

Second, if you are aware of something in your mate's past that continually troubles him, find a biblically trained Christian counselor who can help your mate work through his difficulty. This will not be necessary in every situation, but for some, it could be one of the best investments you could ever make in your mate's self-image.

Third, assure your mate of your "over-acceptance" regardless of what he has done. One of your mate's greatest fears may be that you will find out who he is and what he's done, and then reject him. Your mate's greatest need is to be assured of your steadfast commitment and love. This environment provides a climate for healing and growth.

Be sure to back up your verbal promises of acceptance with actual acceptance. Never throw the past back at your mate. Never. It will only communicate rejection and germinate the seeds of mistrust. Instead, cultivate his self-esteem with your continual acceptance.

Fourth, if he has confessed his past failures to God, help your mate understand that God has forgiven him, so he should not condemn himself. Romans 8:1 says, "There is therefore now no condemnation for those who are in Christ Jesus." Some still condemn themselves, not believing Christ took the punishment we deserve. But when Jesus died on the cross, He paid the price for all our sins — no exceptions. Begin to help your mate understand he should not remain in guilt and self-condemnation. Model that forgiveness by continuing to give it.

Fifth, help your mate understand he has no business remembering that which God has already forgotten. Many Christians live as if they're trying to drive a car by looking through the rearview mirror. Focusing on where they've been, they move forward at a snail's pace, rather than at the brisk velocity God intended. They allow the past to overshadow the present. If this describes your mate, suggest that he put aside the past and allow God to do something new.

One woman had been in a dating relationship she knew was not right. She and her boyfriend had experimented sexually. Finally, she broke off the relationship. During the year that ensued, Isaiah 43:18,19 became very real to her: "Do not call to mind the former things, or ponder things of the past. Behold, I will do something new, now it will spring forth; will you not be aware of it? I will even make a roadway in the wilderness, rivers in the desert." What a promise! Why not encourage your mate to memorize that passage?

Again, Paul writes, "Forgetting what lies behind and reaching forward to what lies ahead, I press on toward the goal for the prize of the upward call of God in Christ Jesus."[4]

Paul wasn't looking in his rearview mirror, even though he had assisted in the murder of Stephen. He was looking forward — at the person of Christ. Help your mate do the same.

Be on Guard Against Unseen Forces

Each of us lives in the midst of an unseen spiritual world that is as real as this book. Just as God with His angels is accomplishing His work on earth, Satan and his demons are seeking to undermine God's work in you and in your mate.

You will encounter some of your most difficult warfare as you begin to build into your mate's life, for it is then that your marriage becomes a threat to what Satan is attempting to do. Satan's plan is diametrically opposed to God's plan. Therefore, Satan wants to discourage and dissolve your mate's self-confidence.

We are not extremists — we are not suggesting a demon is behind every bush — but Satan is a very real enemy, and should be taken seriously. Christ frequently spoke of a personal devil. And consider the following verses:

Peter writes, "Be of sober spirit, be on the alert. Your adversary, the devil, prowls about like a roaring lion, seeking someone to devour."[5] Lions in the forests and plains of Africa prey upon the weak, the unsuspecting and the unprotected, and upon the stragglers who wander from the safety of the herd. Similarly, Satan looks for marriages with weak spots, mates with unprotected self-esteems, spouses living independently of each other. He wants to discourage you from building into your mate. Be advised, and be on the alert.

Paul also admonishes us, "Be strong in the Lord, and in the strength of His might. Put on the full armor of God, that you may be able to stand firm against the schemes of the devil."[6] Paul advises you on how to fight the schemes of the devil: *Be strong in the Lord.* Standing firm in Christ means living obediently. It means believing that what God says is more true than how you feel. Strengthen yourself with faith in God and with prayers.

Remember, "the accuser of the brethren"[7] is at work among Christians, seeking to confuse, discourage and deceive us, and to tempt us to believe a lie instead of the truth about ourselves, our mates and our marriages — all of which affects your mate's self-esteem.

Keep Your Own Attic Clean

We've talked about your mate's past, but what about *your* attic? Is it clean? Is your daily life free from the ridicule of the past? Or are you bitter over something or someone and controlled by anger?

If you feel emotions from the past welling up inside you, consider a project we gave a woman a number of years ago. You may find that completing this project for *yourself* is necessary before you can begin to build your mate's self-image.

Mary was bitter — angry at her parents for the neglect she felt as a child — and at her husband for his inconsistencies. At first she had difficulty admitting her resentment, but finally she did it.

We felt she needed tangible proof that she could put aside her resentment and bitterness, so we assigned her a project.

Alone in her room at home, Mary filled three pages with detailed explanations of how her parents had wronged her and how she was bitter at them. She also listed disappointment after disappointment in her relationship with her husband.

When she finished, she read it aloud. Seeing her anger on paper and hearing it out loud gripped her. It made her cry.

After reading it, Mary bowed her head and prayed through her tears of relief, "Forgive me, God. What I've written here is sin. You've commanded me to honor my parents. I haven't. Instead, I've harbored anger against them for twenty-five years."

She went on, "Forgive me, too, for my lack of a loving spirit toward my husband and my critical attitude toward him."

When she finished, a great relief came over her like a gentle, fresh spring breeze. Mary then took a large red felt-tip pen, and across each of the three pages she printed, in bold letters, the words of 1 John 1:9: "If we confess our sins, He is faithful and righteous to forgive us our sins and to cleanse us from all unrighteousness."

She smiled as she crumpled those sheets of paper. Then, she walked outside, dug a shallow hole in her flower bed, and dropped those three crumpled sheets into it. She lit a match and set the pages on fire. Watching the flame transform the paper to ashes became symbolic of what God was doing in her life. He was transforming something bad into something good.

Then Mary covered the ashes with dirt until the hole was filled, and she piled seven softball-sized rocks on top of that dirt.

Today, when she is tempted to look back at the past and become embittered toward her parents or husband, she looks out her kitchen window and sees her rock pile. It remains there as a refreshing reminder that her past is gone — her sins are forgiven and buried.

What about you? Does your past need to be buried and remembered no more? You'll never be able to build your mate's self-esteem if you are controlled by your past. But once you are free, you can help him recognize and deal with the effects of his past on his self-image.

WHEN TO SEEK PROFESSIONAL COUNSELING

Occasionally outside help or professional counseling may be necessary in order to help your mate get beyond a particular problem. Dr. Frank Minirth, of the Minirth-Meier Clinic in Richardson, Texas, says these half-dozen observations may mean you should encourage your mate to seek a biblically trained outside counselor:

1. *Physical Symptoms*

    An abrupt weight gain or loss in your mate, frequent headaches, or complaints of poor physical health, or a loss of sleep or appetite — any of these could be a signal he needs help.

2. *Mental Symptoms*

    Observed mental anxiety, sadness of appearance, or a confused state of mind could mean qualified help should be sought. A prolonged or frequently repeated depression can be a warning.

3. *Frequent Complaints of Emotional Pain*

    A person who is suffering emotionally through a recent traumatic experience or one who continues having difficulty with an emotional problem from the past should consider getting an opinion from a competent counselor.

4. *Impaired Basic Functioning*

    If he is having a difficult time coping at work, socially, or at home with the most basic responsibilities, it may mean you should seek outside help.

5. *Dependence Upon Drugs or Alcohol*

    Severe feelings of insignificance can result frequently in chemical dependence. These can be accompanied by thoughts of suicide, and they need to be treated by a professional.

6. *Irresponsible Behavior*

    Inconsistent or immoral behavior may mean your mate is not coping well with some internal struggles.

Obviously, if, over a period of time, you feel the problem is much larger than your capability, then you should seek the advice of a trusted counselor who points people to the Scriptures and Christ.

For further information on counseling write:
The Minirth-Meier Clinic
2100 North Collins
Richardson, TX 75080

ESTEEM BUILDER PROJECT

(Use a sheet of paper if necessary.)

1. Do you need to empty out one of the three "corners in your attic"? Parents? Peers? The past in general? Follow the suggestions at the end of the appropriate section to begin the process of healing.

2. Suggest that your mate read this chapter, and then discuss how it may apply to him. Remember: Don't pry; let him share what he feels comfortable about discussing.

3. Perhaps you will want to suggest to your mate that he follow the steps outlined after each section. Be careful not to *push* your mate here.

Planting Positive Words

Your words have the power to contaminate a positive self-image or to heal the spreading malignancy of a negative one.

— 7 —
Words Are Seeds

Building Block 3: Planting Positive Words

LIKE THE AVERAGE American family, we have moved a number of times and have lived in several sections of the United States. We've been homeowners in Boulder, Colorado; San Bernardino, California; Dallas, Texas; and presently in Little Rock, Arkansas.

Our Southern California house came complete with a small, picture-perfect lawn. It was a beauty to behold — the kind of lush, soft green carpet you enjoyed mowing in broad daylight on Saturday morning with your neighbors enviously looking on.

But our other homes had different kinds of lawns. They were also well established, but with weeds. The worst stand of weeds was in Dallas, where we unsuccessfully fought nut grass.

When freshly mowed, our yard of weeds looked pretty . . . from a distance. But within a few days it sent up strange seed pods. The runners, growing unnoticed underground, threatened to choke not only our sparse clumps of grass, but also the few trees we had. We began to suspect this weed had mutated into a new invincible breed, destined to take over the yards of the world. To avoid ridicule, we mowed our lawn at night!

From our experience with lawns, we've learned that weeds come from seeds. Weed seeds primarily come from the soil or a neighbor's yard, or are carried by the wind. It can be a full-time job keeping them at bay. Predictably, we have gained great respect for the potential of seeds.

Words Are Powerful Seeds

Words are like seeds. Once planted in your mate's life, your words will bring forth flowers or weeds, health or disease, healing or poison. You carry a great responsibility for their use. As Proverbs 18:21 says, "Death and life are in the power of the tongue." Your words have the power to contaminate a positive self-image or to heal the spreading malignancy of a negative one.

You are not the only one who plants these seeds in your mate's life. In fact, many of his mistaken perceptions about himself have sprouted from others' negative words. These weed seeds, which have been around since Adam and Eve sinned, have been passed through the soil of humanity. In your mate's lifetime, some have crept across his property lines in the form of jokes, criticism and innuendos from close friends, peers and maybe even you. Others, such as the seeds of the world's values, have been carried by the turbulent winds of our culture and have blown into his thinking. Many have germinated to blight his self-esteem.

While you are not the only source of seeds, as his partner, you have the power to arrest the growth of negative words by sowing your own positive words.

Planting Good Seed

When God created the universe, He used a unique vehicle: words. The Psalmist records how God created all that we see:

"By the *word* of the Lord the heavens were made. For He *spoke,* and it was done; He *commanded,* and it stood fast" (italics added).[1]

Life was conceived in the mind of God and given birth by His words. He could have fashioned creation gently in His hands, yet He chose words. As an all-powerful God, He could have just imagined it into being. But He didn't. He spoke, and it "stood fast."

In a similar way, we share in God's creative handiwork when we use words that give life to our mate's self-esteem. In marriage, one of the most important things about a couple is *what they say to each other.* When positive words flow, the relationship is robust and flourishing. If the lines of understanding and positive communication go down permanently, it is only a matter of time before that marriage dies. We can create life in our mate with our positive words, or we can inflict destruction with our negative or neglectful ones.

Pulling Weeds and Planting Seeds

One of our children's favorite songs is from the children's cassette tape "Ants'hillvania." It is about a prodigal ant, Antony, who became an independ-ant. Through his newly found independence, young Antony left the anthill and went off to do his own thing. He was going to be greater than all the great ants before him: Alex-anter the Great, Michael-ant-gelo, and Napole-ant.

Through various songs and riddles, Antony's friends plead with him to come home. One song, called "Seeds," has application for building your mate's self-esteem. Look at the lyrics and think about what kind of seed you are sowing in your mate.

First you pull the weeds, then you rake and hoe,
Then you plant some seeds, that's the way you sow;
Just you wait and see, everyone will know
What you've planted there, when they start to grow.

Every plant has little seeds
That make others of its kind;
Apple seeds make apple trees,
And they'll do it every time.

Seeds make flowers and shrubs and trees,

Seeds make ferns and vines and weeds.
What you plant is what you grow,
So be careful what you sow.[2]

Antony concludes he's been sowing the wrong seed in
his independence. The cute little parable ends as he becomes
a repent-ant and decides to come home. His family, thrilled
that the prodigal ant has come home, kills the fatted aphid,
has a feast and lives happily ever after.

Sow the Right Seed; Avoid the Bad

Like Antony, your mate may need a good word. Proverbs
12:25 says, "Anxiety in the heart of a man weighs it down,
but a good word makes it glad." Notice the impact of a "good
word." Not a sentence or a paragraph. Not a message. Just
one, well-placed, positive word.

Be sure to appreciate the power of words. They can
assault our mates or honor them as valuable people with
God-given assets. Efforts to understand the past and give
unconditional acceptance will be quickly negated if we sow
pessimistic, critical or unsympathetic words into our mate's
heart. The Living Bible says it well: "Evil words destroy. Godly
skill [wisdom] rebuilds" (Proverbs 11:9).

Heed the warning of the children's song:

You must choose your seeds with care;
What you sow will blossom there. . . .
What you plant is what you grow,
So be careful what you sow.[3]

Choose with wisdom and care the words you speak to
your spouse. They are critical to his self-esteem, for in them
he sees himself.

One final warning on weed seeds: Don't expect an immediate "crop failure" of weeds if you've been planting negative
words in your mate's life for years. Asking your mate's forgiveness may hasten the process of killing the weeds, but the seed-
lings of carelessly spoken words may take years to die out.
Ask God to make you mindful of the power of your tongue
and to make you more aware of the words you speak to your
mate.

Words, however, are not the only source for weed seeds. Your negative attitudes toward your mate also have a devastating effect on his self-image. Non-verbal cues or ignoring your mate can plant seeds, too. You may be habitually sowing negative words or attitudes without realizing it.

But remember, God delights in changing lives and in giving new beginnings. Your marriage can become a healthy productive garden where two people generously express to one another gratitude, appreciation, belief and praise.

Sow Words of Praise

Carefully read this definition of praise: "to give value, to lift up, to extol, to magnify, to honor, to commend, to applaud." If you give some creative thought and time to the words in that definition, you could come up with literally hundreds of ways to praise your mate. Since building your mate's self-esteem is basically a matter of helping him feel valuable, praise is a necessary tool for that process. The more you verbally express your appreciation (praise), the more secure your mate will become in his self-esteem.

Everyone loves to be praised; your mate is no exception. William James wrote, "The deepest principle in human nature is the craving to be appreciated." Mark Twain said, "I can live for two months on a good compliment."

Have you ever asked someone to repeat a compliment? We have. "Oh, you really liked our Family Life Conference? Tell us what meant the most to you." Inwardly we are saying, "Yes, we needed that, but would you tell us one more time so we can relish your comments for a few seconds longer?" Life can seem intolerably heavy at times, and a good word can help lighten the load.

Arnold Glascow has said, "Praise does wonders for our sense of hearing." It also does wonders for your sense of sight. When you praise another person, you take your eyes off yourself and focus on someone else for a few brief moments. This positive focus on another not only helps put his life in perspective, but yours as well.

HOW TO PRAISE YOUR MATE

1. Praise specifically.

Give your mate value and honor through the gift of praise. Your mate needs you to praise him specifically for who he is as a person. This helps him see his uniqueness. He also needs praise for those things he does — his effort and work — for you and for your family's benefit. Sow the good seed of praise in his life with statements such as:

"I appreciate you because you . . ."

"I admire you for your . . ."

"Thank you for . . ."

To appreciate means "to raise in value," while to depreciate means "to lower in value." You can watch your mate's value appreciate because of your verbal appreciation of him!

Think about it for a moment. What do you really appreciate about your mate that you haven't said "thank you" for in a while? What good qualities, good deeds, or good attitudes can you think of? Take a minute or two right now and list five. Make them as specific as possible. And why not share them at your next meal together? Praise not only is "becoming," it is infectious — others might join in.

Husband: Wife:

_____   _____
_____   _____
_____   _____
_____   _____
_____   _____

Don't forget to praise your mate for those mundane daily duties. Tell him *why* you appreciate the tasks he performs; tell him how you benefit from the little (or big) things he does. Make a mental note of those unpleasant, difficult tasks, and give a verbal reward of encouragement the next time he does one. It can motivate him to keep on and to try again.

Any time Dennis fixes something around the house, I (Barbara) am quick to express my appreciation. (I know how inept he feels in this area and what it takes for him to crank

up the courage to at least try.) I also thank him often for working hard and providing for us as a family.

Robert Louis Stevenson said, "Make the most of the best
and the least of the worst." Far too often we reverse what
Stevenson said, but if you follow this advice, you will inspire
your mate to keep on trying, and you will bring out his best.

2. Praise wisely and truthfully.

When a marriage relationship hits a trouble spot, whether
small and brief or large and prolonged, it's difficult to find
much to praise. Yet those are the times we need it most. So
initiate giving your mate praise. Bring relief to him in the
midst of trouble.

Solomon wrote, "The words of wise men are like goads,
and masters of these collections are like well-driven nails."[4]
When you choose to give positive encouragement and praise
to your mate, your words can prod or goad him in the right
direction. Your wise and truthful words will bring perspective
to his life, your relationship, and your situation as a couple.
Finding a solution may even be easier.

"But what if all this praise goes to my mate's head?"
you may be asking. "Won't he become prideful?" There is a
difference between truthful praise and flattery. Flattery gratifies
a person's vanity. It can notice and compliment *only* a person's
physical looks, intelligence, or wealth. Praise, however, is
based on a person's character and deeds. When you truthfully
praise and applaud his godly choices, you inspire him to go
deeper still in his character, which is the root from which his
performance should grow.

Paul exhorts, "Speak truth, each one of you, with his
neighbor."[5] At the center of these words is "truth." Once again
we find the standard for bringing value to another. Truth results
in assurance and security, worth and value. It becomes the
compass in the storm, confidently steering us in the right
direction.

Praise your mate in all situations, using wisdom to meet
the need of the moment, and speaking truthfully to construct
his character.

3. Praise generously.

Your praise can be excessive only if your words are
insincere. Genuine, heartfelt praise cannot be overdone. Besides,

your mate gets plenty of criticism and correction from others and from himself to keep it in balance. And if he does get a big head, God is fully capable of shrinking it back to normal.

In the early months of our marriage, we spontaneously complimented and praised each other for newly discovered characteristics we liked. It became almost a game to see who could find another good quality to praise. We named our exclusive "club" the Mutual Admiration Society. It remained quite active for several years and provided much of the basis for the great beginning of our marriage.

Today, it's not quite the same with a houseful of children and new discoveries about one another coming less frequently. But, some evenings at the dinner table, the Mutual Admiration Society reconvenes. A question is raised, such as, "What do you appreciate most about Dad?" We then go around the table. We've heard some classic, and truthful, comments, such as: "He goes fishing with me"; "He goes on dates with me"; or, from our five-year-old Rebecca, "He sneaks chocolate with me." It's very difficult to be depressed after a chorus of youngsters, who are mostly blind to your faults, cheer you on.

William James said, "All of us, in the glow of feeling we have pleased, want to do more to please." Thus, you can motivate your mate to excellence in his character and his performance with generous, liberal, fervent praise.

Sow Words of Belief

In this self-centered culture in which we live, rarely will you find others who unequivocally believe in your mate. You have the main responsibility for sowing words of belief in your spouse.

One of the strengths Dennis brought into our marriage was a steady belief in me (Barbara). When I am tempted to become overwhelmed by self-doubt, he rarely, if ever, joins me in my verbal self-deprecating accusations. Instead. he reminds me of the truth. He tells me what he thinks about me, positively, of course, without lying and without flattery. He also praises me for the things I do right. His words help turn my focus from a negative view of self to a positive one. His unwavering belief in me has given me the much-needed confidence I lacked in my self-esteem.

Words that communicate belief are important to your mate's self-image. He needs your unparalleled belief in him. You have been drafted to play on his team, to be the coach who believes in him, and to be the cheerleader who gives praise even when he loses. He needs you to be his biggest fan, not his sharpest critic.

Your mate will become the person you tell him he is. It's the mirror principle again. Words create images; they direct behavior. Your words influence what he expects out of himself.

One woman we know uses words extremely well. Recently, when her husband was in the middle of some pressure-packed situations at work, her believing words of reassurance kept him going. "You're all right. I believe in you. I'm confident you will make the right decision," she assured him. "These times will pass soon. I'm ready to talk about it any time and help in any way I can."

Expressing belief in your mate assures him of your faith in him as a person and in his ability to perform in your marriage, your family, and his job. Words of belief tell him he is trusted. He will be motivated to prove himself worthy of your trust.

Jesus taught in Matthew 13:3-8 that the gospel falls on many types of soil. Similarly, seeds of praise can fall on many types of soil. Your mate's soil might welcome and soak up your praises, or it may be hardened from years of hearing negative words, and be unable to receive your words of praise and belief. Be patient. Try to understand why his soil is as it is. Ask yourself: What specific factors have affected my mate's soil? Even good seed planted at the wrong time or under poor conditions (negative attitudes) will not produce outstanding crops.

Weeds or Fruit Trees: Take Your Pick

A few years ago, we took a fall vacation to New England. One frosty morning, we picked apples for five dollars a bushel. The "pick your own" orchard of mature Cortland apple trees covered the rolling hills like a green calico patchwork quilt stitched in rows. The limbs were heavily laden with the ruby-red fruit, which we picked and ate for the better part of two hours that crisp, cloudy fall morning.

As we were leaving, we met the owner of the orchard. We complimented him on the condition of his trees and their delicious white, crisp fruit. He received our praise, but was quick to add his vantage point. He told us he had endured bitter New England winters, and had fought bugs and weeds for years to get the orchard to its present productivity and profitability. It had taken hard work and perseverance, but it was beginning to pay off.

In a similar way, you have been entrusted with a plot of soil: your mate. You also have been given seeds: your words. The choices you make today — to plant good seed in your mate and to avoid bad seed — will guarantee a harvest someday. You must weather the onslaught of changing circumstances, unexpected difficulties and life in general as you love and live with him. But faithful care will result in the roots of his self-esteem going down deeply into the truth of God's Word.

Paul writes in Galatians 6:9, "And let us not lose heart in doing good, for in due time we shall reap if we do not grow weary." That's quite a promise. You will reap a good harvest if you don't grow weary and quit, but the kind of harvest really depends upon you. Weeds or fruit trees, take your pick.

ESTEEM BUILDER PROJECT

(Use a sheet of paper if necessary.)

1. Write a paragraph or a letter of positive words to your mate. Pick one of the topics below:
   - A letter of praise
   - A letter of appreciation
   - A letter of encouragement
   - A statement of belief
2. Be specific — avoid generalities.
3. Read it to your mate before going to bed tonight.

Constructing in Difficult Times

Weather the storms of life by turning toward one another and building into each other rather than rejecting each other.

— 8 —
Building in the Storm

- Life's Difficulties Can Erode Your Mate's Self-Confidence
- Suffering Is Universal
- Tragedy Threatens to Shatter Self-Esteem
- Daily Stress Attempts to Undermine Self-Esteem
- Building Your Mate in a Storm
- Weather the Storms Together
- Esteem Builder Project

Building Block 4: Constructing in Difficult Times

FOR SOME REASON that only God knows, I (Dennis) did not leave for work on time that June morning. I had just finished tying my tie as Barbara began doing her exercises. Suddenly, I noticed she had stopped and was sitting on the bed with her head between her knees.

"Are you O.K.?" I asked.

"No, I don't think so," Barbara said weakly. "I feel like I'm going to faint."

Since her pulse was high from the exercise, she rested a few minutes, waiting for her heartbeat to return to normal. I had experienced an abnormally high heartbeat that winter, so when her rapid heartbeat failed to slow down, I assured her I knew exactly what to do. I put my arm around her and suggested she get up and walk around with me.

After I helped her up, Barbara took only a couple of steps before turning around, collapsing on the bed, and nearly losing consciousness. When she complained again that her heart was really pounding, I began to get frightened.

I placed my fingers against her neck and attempted to check her pulse, but Barbara's heart was racing so fast I was unable to count the beats. "I'm calling an ambulance," I told her.

I called a neighbor to take care of our two small children. The ambulance arrived and then rushed us to the hospital.

The heart monitor at the hospital told the story: Barbara's heart was pounding at three hundred beats per minute. For the next six hours, the medical team did all they could. Barbara's bed in the coronary intensive care area literally shook from her heart beating so hard. Her pulse remained unchanged.

I had begun praying for Barbara the moment I recognized her problem, but I felt so powerless. So I called Kitty Longstreth, a widow who had become a close friend, and asked her to pray and call others who would also. Shortly after noon, "Miss Kitty" (as she is affectionately known to the Rainey family and many others) got down on her knees and started praying for Barbara.

I was allowed to see Barbara once every two hours, and then only for five minutes, so I had plenty of time to pray, read the Scriptures and think. I recall wondering early that afternoon, "What would I do with two small children under three years of age?" Those were grim moments in both our lives.

At 2 P.M., Barbara's lungs started to fill with fluid. At five beats per second, her heart did not have time to fill up with blood and completely pump it out, so her blood pressure was dangerously low. At 3 o'clock she began to have difficulty breathing.

The doctors warned me that now, more than ever, coronary failure was a very real possibility. At 4 P.M., the cardiologist began preparations to use electric shock to stop her heart, and hopefully restart it at its normal rate.

But they didn't have to. Miss Kitty, who had been faithfully praying over Barbara's life, finally felt the freedom from the Lord to get up off her knees. She later told me she *knew* everything was O.K.

"I knew that either Barbara had died and gone to be with the Lord or her heart rate had returned to normal," Miss Kitty said. "God gave me a peace to stop praying." Her clock read a few minutes past 4.

The doctors told me they never had to use electric shock because Barbara's heart rate reverted to normal "on its own." The time was 4:05 P.M.

Although a previously undiscovered congenital heart defect was still present, the doctors gave us some hope that Barbara would lead a long, normal life. They released her from the hospital five days later.

For the next month, Barbara understandably became very introspective about anything that was going on in her body. She suddenly was acutely aware of every heartbeat and physical ache.

Then we found out she was pregnant.

In the next eight months, we learned to live with questions — questions about two people, a mother and a baby, rather than just Barbara. These were heavy, thought-provoking months. There was little romance, little laughter, and little emotion left for anything or anyone else. It was an oppressive time, especially for Barbara.

Life's Difficulties Can Erode Your Mate's Self-Confidence

When we said our marriage vows, neither of us thought we'd have a year of suffering like that one we experienced in 1977. Today we are more realistic about life. We have learned that suffering comes to all of us at different times in our lives. We also have seen that one's self-image becomes fragile when the storms of life strike.

For us, Barbara's introspection over her health was at times overwhelming. Occasionally, I wanted to tell her to "just move on." I felt she was too preoccupied. I wanted somehow to let her know that the children and I needed her to be with us — mentally, as well as physically.

Most important, however, was how all this affected Barbara's self-image. Suddenly faced with her own mortality, she felt expendable. She felt discouraged at her inability to "rise above" her circumstances. A confident self-image is largely dependent on that feeling of being needed — of having something to offer — and one's personal ability to perform. With both of those pillars shaken, Barbara entered a state of bewilderment and discouragement.

She became a little fatalistic about life. And although we knew God was still sovereignly in control of all that had occurred in our lives, we had to reckon with these disturbing thoughts. Together we moved through this time.

After nine months, Barbara gave birth to Samuel, a healthy, nine-pound-five-ounce boy. It was God's signal to us that there was hope for the future.

Suffering Is Universal

God is gracious and doesn't often allow couples to experience suffering as Job did, but He does allow measured doses of trouble at sovereignly ordained intervals. We watched dear friends of ours bury their seven-year-old boy two days before Christmas. We have helped others in business disasters and job losses. Other couples we know have experienced suffering from infertility, repeated illnesses, aging, mid-life crises, problems with parents, teenage rebellion, death of parents, financial setbacks, grown children getting divorced, or children disgracing their family's name.

All of these people have experienced loss. Some have endured earth-shaking blows. Many, if not all, questioned their self-worth and self-confidence. The difficulties produced strength in many, while others have never quite seemed to recover.

Tragedy Threatens to Shatter Self-Esteem

It was already hot that Texas summer morning when Dave met early with a land developer to talk about a zoning issue. It was August 25, 1977, a day that neither he nor his wife, Carol, would ever forget. She had left her two boys — Ben, almost twelve, and Tom, eight — at home to play while she ran to school to prepare for a class that she would begin teaching the following week.

Dave finished his meeting with the land developer and almost stopped by his home, but he decided against it and drove on to work.

The boys had been playing with their dad's deer rifle the night before, and, finding a shell, they had put it in the chamber, just to pretend. That morning when they decided to play with the rifle again, they forgot about that shell, still in the chamber. The gun went off and eight-year-old Tom was killed instantly.

The days, weeks and months that followed were characterized not only by emotional pain and grief, but by physical pain as well. Dave said he felt as if a hay hook had been sunk into his stomach and then ripped out. Carol fell into deep introspection. Both asked, "Why?"

Unlike many couples who experience a tragedy of that magnitude, they moved through that loss and today have a strong marriage. Their stability and strength came as they built into one another's lives through prayer and complete dependence upon Jesus Christ.

Dave prayed daily for Carol and for himself. He prayed for understanding of his wife and for knowledge of how to help her. He renewed his commitment to her and pledged a renewal of their wedding vows. She knew he had resolutely decided to endure and persevere. She felt deeply cared for. He helped her look to the future, without pushing or being impatient with her.

Carol spent enormous amounts of time reading the Bible and shared these scriptures with Dave. She focused on the things that were "worthy of praise"[1] and expressed them to Dave and Ben. Although it took nearly all the energy she had, she sought to make dinner a happy time. And she started exercising with Dave — it relieved the stress and gave them time to think and talk.

As a couple, they forced themselves to focus on others and their church involvement. Together they wrapped their arms of love around Ben and helped him work through his grief in his own timing. Above all else, their commitment to Jesus Christ and to one another has been strengthened beyond measure. They have built each other and their home upon the "Rock."[2]

Daily Stress Attempts to Undermine Self-Esteem

Though the magnitude of this couple's suffering does not strike repeatedly over one's lifetime, we are likely to experience painful times in our lives when we are forced to hold on to God and to each other for our survival. These times hit like a flash flood, without warning.

But suffering is not limited to times of tragedy. Affliction, heartache and trouble visit almost predictably at different stages of life, usually during times of change and stress. One occupation with plenty of scheduled and unscheduled trials is the job of being a mother.

The average mother today is seldom esteemed by society for her contribution to the next generation. Instead she is told mothering is a menial task that anyone could do.

Without feeling esteem in her role, she is often unprepared and worn out when her children hit adolescence. Most teenagers are not gentle on their mothers. Instead, they have a way of questioning parental decisions, judgments and authority on almost every issue. And most teenagers are impervious as to how their attitudes and actions chip away their mother's self-esteem. Meanwhile, the mother feels attacked in this battle of the wills and finds herself questioning her worth and value.

If you are a husband and father, come alongside your wife to protect, esteem and support her. Crossing the turbulent waters of child-raising together will strengthen your mate's self-confidence and bring you to the empty nest united.

Building Your Mate in a Storm

The storms of life will affect you and your mate differently. You may be tempted to turn away from one another. Don't! Instead, turn toward one another in total commitment and provide a shelter in the storm.

Give your mate the freedom to process what's going on in his life. Don't expect him to flip a switch and just "deal with the problem" and then "move on." It's not usually that easy. And if your mate's suffering doesn't go away after a reasonable time, resist the temptation to make statements such as:

"Snap out of it! Trust God!"

"Quit acting like a big baby! You're more mature than that!"

"We've spent enough time talking about this. I think it's time we just put the whole matter to rest."

We've found that to arrive at the end product that God wants in our lives, we must go through a lifetime process of becoming like Christ. God wants to get our attention, and He sometimes must take radical action. When we won't listen to all He is saying, the heat is turned up rather than off.

Here is where your mate's self-esteem can benefit from a large measure of your understanding and longsuffering. True

love doesn't quit just because its object doesn't respond fast
enough.

Find out what your mate needs. We have discovered in
our relationship that it is best to simply ask, "I want to meet
your needs and be the best possible partner I can be, but at
times I don't know how. Would you tell me how you want me
to love and encourage you in this situation?"

Your mate *may* be looking for a solution to a problem.
For example, if you have a difficult child, your wife wants
your participation. She desires you to join forces with her in
loving and disciplining the child. In other situations as well,
your active involvement in problem-solving may be just the
encouragement your mate longs for.

Possibly your mate doesn't want any advice, but instead
would like you to come alongside and listen compassionately.
After you've listened and listened, it may be appropriate to
say to your mate, "You're O.K. You're going to make it,
because I know you will ultimately do what's right. I believe
in you. And I'm praying for you."

*You can build your mate's confidence during these times
by offering perspective.* The preacher in Ecclesiastes penned
these famous words, "There is an appointed time for everything.
And there is a time for every event under heaven — a time
to give birth, and a time to die . . . a time to weep, and a
time to laugh; a time to mourn, and a time to dance."[3]

Perspective is gained by looking up from the stones and
boulders that are tripping your mate along the way, in order
to see the whole panorama of life. Use your words to lift life's
pains up against the backdrop of God's sovereign control. All
that happens in life is sifted through the all-knowing, all-loving
hands of God. Recognizing that may not make the pain any
less intense for your mate, but it will offer hope for the future.

Bring balance to your mate's assessment of his own life
by recalling God's faithfulness in the past. Point out, too, that
he is valuable, although he can be tempted to feel otherwise
in the midst of difficulty. If he is suffering for doing wrong,
direct him to the graciousness of a God who wants to forgive
our worst mistakes.

Our perspective of circumstances is aided when the Scriptures permeate our thinking. Often our ears are more keenly
tuned to hear God's voice in difficult times. Your mate's spirit

may be lifted if you read an extended portion of Scripture (such as Psalm 23, 31 or 34) to him at the end of a heavy day. At other times, a verse or your own paraphrase of the truth can bring light where darkness has enveloped him.

Ecclesiastes 3:7b says there is "a time to be silent, and a time to speak." Depend upon God to give you the wisdom to know when to be silent, when to speak, and what words to use to bring perspective to your mate. God promises to give wisdom if we will ask in faith.[4] One of the greatest feelings of satisfaction comes from knowing that God has given you the right word at the right moment for your spouse. And He *will* do just that.

For Christians, suffering precedes fruitfulness.[5] One prerequisite of bearing fruit in the Christian life is the painful process of "pruning." Jesus said, "Every branch that bears fruit, He prunes it, that it may bear more fruit."[6] God is lovingly ordering events, circumstances and relationships in our lives for the purpose of our becoming more and more like Jesus Christ. Personal godliness is His goal for us. The pruning He must do seems at times to be severe — even too painful to bear. But there is little fruitfulness without pruning.

One of the great privileges of marriage is that we do not have to go through these pruning periods alone. God has provided a partner with whom we can share the pain of the process. If your mate is in the midst of a season of pruning, come alongside him and remind him of the hope of becoming more Christlike through suffering.

One final suggestion is to avoid becoming isolated from one another during the storms of life. Marriage is the process of becoming one flesh, yet suffering can be a lonely, solitary experience. One natural tendency is to withdraw from others, especially your mate, if you do not feel understood. A second is to lash out in anger and frustration at those most loved. Both actions result in isolation and can destroy your mate's self-worth.

Aggressively make your relationship with your mate a priority during times of strain and struggle. Build into your schedule time to talk. If possible, take walks together. Schedule a weekend to get away and minister to your mate in his area of personal struggle. You may wish to work together on solving the problem, if that's possible.

Above all else, pursue your mate. Don't let him become isolated by the crisis. It affects you both.

Weather the Storms Together

A little girl was sitting on her grandpa's lap getting sage advice. As her blue eyes peered deeply into his, the elderly, silver-haired man said, "Sweetheart, remember, life is like licking honey off a thorn."

It's true. Life is bittersweet, but the hope for your mate and you is not having to "go it alone." God has called you to weather the storms together. So build into your mate's life, that the world might see Jesus Christ more clearly in his life and yours. And remember, as Ray Stedman, pastor and author, says, "The ship won't sink and the storm won't last forever."

ESTEEM BUILDER PROJECT

(Use a sheet of paper if necessary.)

1. Is your mate presently being pulled down by something you are not sharing together? Why not tell him you want to be a part of this time in his life and be the person he needs you to be?
2. Discuss with your mate what he needs from you:
   a. Help with a solution
   b. Compassion, patience and understanding in the process
   c. The perspective that truth provides
   d. A reminder of God's provision from the past
3. Today, begin to ask God to help you pursue your mate and know exactly what to say and do to build into his life.

Giving the Freedom to Fail

Release your mate from the prison of performance with the golden key labeled "the freedom to fail."

— 9 —
Down But Not Out
for the Count

- Hope for Your Mate
- Failure's Effects
- An Anatomy of Failure
- Why We Fail
- "It's O.K.! Everybody Makes Mistakes"
- The Antidote for Those Who Fail — Six Gifts
  - The Gift of Compassion
  - The Gift of Continual Affirmation
  - The Gift of Perspective
  - The Gift of Disassociation
  - The Gift of Encouraging Decisive Living
  - The Gift of Forgiveness
- Esteem Builder Project

Building Block 5: Giving the Freedom to Fail

HAVE YOU EVER wondered why your mate:

- Finds failing so threatening, and even frightening?
- Has difficulty admitting that he's wrong or that he has failed?
- Is paralyzed at times by the fear of failure?
- Experiences internal feelings of failure, despite outward appearances of success?

If you answered yes to any of the above questions, you are seeing the symptoms of an insecure individual who has difficulty dealing with failure. Your mate isn't alone. All of us are prone to fail, and no marriage is exempt from its influence. Making mistakes and experiencing failure are predictable. We don't like it — it's not fun — but we do fail.

In a performance-oriented culture such as ours, failures hit us like a punch in the stomach. Repeated failures often result in a knockout blow, and many give up. Emotionally, failure is extremely costly. It leaves your mate with feelings of guilt, self-condemnation and doubt. It's no wonder that failure is feared and risk is so frightening.

Hope for Your Mate

Perhaps your mate has been shattered by past failures and, consequently, has a fragile self-image. By slowly forging the freedom to fail into your mate, you'll help him become more open to change, more willing to take risks, and more confident in decision making.

Giving your mate the freedom to fail communicates to him that you are on his team . . . regardless. It tells him that even if he makes a mistake and falls, you will be there to help him up, dust him off, and encourage him to try again. The issue is not whether he will ever fail, but rather, will he get back up, and will you be at his side? In an address to a nation divided by the Civil War, Abraham Lincoln underscored the need to persevere. He said, "I am not concerned that you have fallen. I am concerned that you arise."

Failure's Effects

Failure is a strict taskmaster and it accompanies us all too frequently in the journey of life.

After failing, we usually attempt to avoid any future mistakes by walking one of two paths. The most commonly followed path is accelerated performance. Our failures motivate us to stay ahead of impending disasters. The fear of failure is like a shadow on our heels, threatening to overtake us. On the basis of our success in avoiding failures, we erroneously conclude that our worth or value is rooted solely in our performance.

The other path is the way of resignation or passivity. W. C. Fields once quipped, "If at first you don't succeed, then quit. There's no use in being a fool about it." The price of failure is too high: disapproval, anger, imposed guilt, ridicule and rejection. So we avoid any unnecessary risks. A life with no risk *appears* to offer safety and security, but *delivers* guilt, boredom, further apathy, and even lower feelings of self-esteem.

An Anatomy of Failure

We find an anatomy of failure in the life of Moses. Exodus 3 begins with Moses exiled by his failure. He had just murdered an Egyptian and, fearing for his life, he fled from Pharaoh into the wilderness.

For forty years, Moses lived a life of exile in the desert, undoubtedly hounded by a host of condemning voices that reminded him he had been rejected by the Jewish nation as well as his adopted Egyptian family. When God came to him in the burning bush, Moses was struggling with an identity problem — the result of his failure, rejection and forty years of being an alien in the desert. He was full of self-doubt.

God told Moses He was going to send him to free the Israelites, to which Moses responded, "Who am I . . .?"[1] God simply said, "I will be with you."[2] Above all, Moses needed God's reassuring presence. Without Him, Moses never could stand before Pharaoh. The rejection would be too painful. Left alone, he was certain to fail.

Moses' next question was, "Who are you? What is the name of the one who sends me?"[3] God graciously responded. Even though he told Moses who He was, Moses again resisted His command and listened to the nagging voices of self-doubt. Exodus 4:1 reveals Moses' feelings of uncertainty: "What if they will not believe me, or listen to what I say?" God then gave Moses two signs of His divine presence. First, He transformed Moses' staff into a serpent. The second sign was the instant affliction of Moses' hand with leprosy and its equally instantaneous and miraculous restoration. These two "visual aids" were embedded in Moses' memory to remind him that God's presence was powerful and transforming. God *was* with him.

In spite of these convincing and powerful displays of God's omnipotence, Moses' feelings of inadequacy resurfaced: "Please, Lord, I have never been eloquent, neither recently nor in time past, nor since Thou hast spoken to Thy servant; for I am slow of speech and slow of tongue."[4] God reminded Moses who made his mouth. He told Moses He would teach him what to say.

After all this dialogue with God, Moses dared to make one more response, the essence of which was, "I can't do what

You've asked. Please choose someone else."[5] Rather than focusing on God, Moses focused on himself. He was like the little boy in the school play whose one line was, "It is I, be not afraid." But when the night of the play came, the boy came out on stage and exclaimed, "It's me and I'm scared."

Only when Moses saw there was no way out did he submit to God's call. He was so convinced of his own worthlessness that it took time for God to convince him otherwise.

Your mate also may have a difficult time believing God and you. He, too, may be plagued by failure. His failure may not have been murder, as Moses' was, but it may be one of dozens of experiences that can whisper "you're a failure" in his ear, such as:

- continued rejection (or lack of approval) by a family member
- a broken friendship
- a lost job
- feeling personal rejection at work
- perpetual unemployment
- an idea that didn't work
- a bad investment
- a strained relationship
- accusations by a child
- words that can't be taken back, spoken in anger
- marital unfaithfulness
- a previous divorce
- having lashed out at a child in anger
- a foolish mistake

Note that in this chapter of Moses's life, part of God's solution to Moses' self-worth problem was a companion: Aaron. They became a team. Undoubtedly, Aaron frequently reminded Moses of the truth: that he was God's man for the assignment and that God would be faithful to His promises. Just as Moses needed Aaron, your mate needs you.

Why We Fail

Failure comes from not reaching standards — God's, ours and others'. We fail because we are human. Failure is a part of the flawed fabric of our humanity.

At our house we experience plenty of failure, both big and small. For instance, a meal without a spill is nothing short of miraculous. The milk may go shooting across the supper table or form a lazy river that cascades over the edge, splattering on the floor. We've had some classic spills: two simultaneously, four at one sitting, and one that spilled perfectly into Dennis's shoe (while he was wearing it). Our favorite phrase for the children has become, "It's O.K. Everybody makes mistakes."

The other evening at dinner, I (Dennis) spilled my drink. A little hand patted my arm, and Rebecca (our five-year-old) reassuringly said, "It's O.K., Dad. Everybody makes mistakes."

As Christians, we are acutely aware of our shortcomings and failures because of our relationship with a perfect, righteous, and blameless God. Frequently, other Christians, too, are quick to inform us when we fail!

It's comforting to know we are not alone — others have needed and claimed God's forgiveness when they failed. King David failed through his adulterous relationship with Bathsheba and the murder of her husband. Peter failed by denying Christ. Thomas doubted, and Saul (Paul) assisted in the murder of Stephen.

Yet none of these lives represented total failure. They sought forgiveness. They didn't give up. They kept on. Faithfulness in spite of personal foul-ups was their track record.

Sometimes people "fail" because they set their expectations too high, or they let others' — including their mate's — unrealistic expectations become their standard.

Do you recall going to the circus or watching on television an entertainer perform with trained dogs that jumped through hoops? The most unlikely dog, a tiny one, would jump through the hoop just when you knew there was no way that little fellow could possibly leap that high. The trainer knew what to expect out of his performers, and, to the crowd's delight, that little dog always succeeded.

Unlike that trainer, some spouses haven't studied and worked with their mates enough to know their limits and potential abilities. Or if they have determined what they are capable of, they don't like what they see. Others keep raising "the hoops" higher and higher for them to jump through. When they find the point they can't reach, they react with, "I knew you couldn't do it," or "I can't believe you can't do this; it's so easy." They conclude that their mates are failures in this area, and they let them know it.

Have you held up hoops for your mate? Ask God to show you any areas in which you are contributing to your mate's feelings of failure. Be sure you're not part of the problem, so you can be part of the solution.

What is the solution for the fear of failure? How do you encourage a partner whose feelings of failure are triggered by the most insignificant of circumstances?

The Antidote for Those Who Fail

One of the most powerful principles we've experienced in building one another's self-image is:

GIVE YOUR MATE THE FREEDOM TO FAIL.

When you give your mate the freedom to fail, you begin to remove the pressure to perform for acceptance. You also free him to excel. He is free to take risks and to try again. Failure becomes a tutor, and not a judge. We learn from failures instead of being intimidated by them. And in the absence of condemnation, self-worth swells.

For years, we talked of moving to the country. The thought of the children having room to roam sounded inviting, but moving a large family is a chore. And, more important, it was a risk. What if we didn't like driving back and forth to town? What if we didn't like being so isolated from friends? So, the decision was put off. For some reason, the risk seemed too great.

Then, one day Barbara said, "So what if we decide we don't like it? We can sell and move back to town!" Her statement clicked; it gave me (Dennis) the freedom to make a decision — even a wrong one! So we decided to try it, and we love it! But the decision came only after the fear of failure was removed.

You may be asking, "How can I give my mate the freedom to fail?" We would like to recommend six gifts you can give your mate which will begin to release him from the fear of failure. These gifts can slowly take away the fear of failure and, with it, the fear of rejection. Keep in mind that you, too, will possibly fail by taking some of these gifts back. That's O.K. Failure is a part of learning, for both of you.

The Gift of Compassion

In chapter six, we discussed how the past has power over a person's life. Perhaps your mate is overly cautious and has difficulty with change or making decisions. Most likely, much of this fearfulness has been ingrained in him for years. He needs your compassion and patience as he begins to take risks.

Every person's life has a context. The more you fully grasp the context of your mate's journey to adulthood and then express compassion, the more freedom your mate will feel to admit failures to you. Compassion says, "I share your feelings."

During his childhood, your mate may not have experienced a relationship in which he had freedom to fail. Perhaps his many failures taught him to expect such reactions as rejection, disapproval and anger from those over him. He learned to feel that he deserved rejection, that rejection "is the natural consequence of failure." Parents, coaches, teachers, peers, boyfriends and girlfriends, siblings, and other significant people gave him a personal heritage of either success or failure.

Whatever his background, your mate needs your compassionate, consistent and tireless belief in him. Talk about the context of his life and together gain understanding of those past mistakes, along with the present ones. Don't leave your mate alone to deal with his failures. Tell him you are unlike those who rejected him; your commitment is unwavering and your love is consistent, despite his imperfections. In the climate of compassion and patience, he will begin to feel free to take risks and fail without fear of rejection.

 The Gift of Continual Affirmation

Recently, Barbara drove to the grocery store and accidentally backed our van into a couple's newly painted Camaro, denting it slightly. Understandably, they were not very happy about it and insisted on calling the county sheriff's office to come file an accident report. I (Dennis) joined Barbara at the store and, while she waited for the police to arrive, I assured her that everything would be fine — that in the end it didn't really matter.

We both knew she had made a mistake, but it would have done no good at that point to drive home a moral lesson or give her some driving tips. She needed reassurance. She needed to know she was all right and that I was not angry with her. Did it help? Here's what she says:

> I felt so foolish for having dented that car. I was in a hurry and mentally preoccupied as I walked to our van. As I climbed in and shut the door, I didn't see the car behind me, but it was there. I had failed to look, and my apologies didn't make the dent go away.
>
> I wondered what Dennis would think and say. I was pretty sure he wouldn't be upset with me, but I speculated mentally for a while. I needed to experience his approval in this new situation, and I did. I was affirmed again, and like pieces of a puzzle coming together, I feel I am gaining more and more freedom to make mistakes.

The gift of continual affirmation creates the environment where another can fail. It reminds your mate daily that he is worthy and not a "dummy" if he makes an error. And if your mate is not condemned for his failures, he will learn from them. Henry Ward Beecher wrote, "Compassion will cure more sins than condemnation." One of our favorite verses, 1 Peter 4:8, says, "Love covers a multitude of sins." Continuous, ongoing, unbroken approval in the face of the many mistakes and failures of life will build your mate's self-esteem.

 The Gift of Perspective

Jesus said, "You shall know the truth, and the truth shall make you free."[6] As partners in the pilgrimage of life, we are responsible to speak the truth to one another to help balance our perspective of failure.

Understanding the truth of God's sovereign rule, that He is in control, brings an eternal view to your mate's mistakes. The promise of Romans 8:28 (KJV), "All things work together for good," beautifully illustrates His absolute supremacy. Those words offer comfort, reminding us that God can use our mistakes and failures. Nothing is wasted in His economy. Encourage your mate to believe God and, as a couple, ask Him to use your failures for good.

Another view you can give your mate is that most failures are not as big as they appear in our minds. Help him see the overall picture. Mistakes are not that monumental when seen against the backdrop of a whole life.

 The Gift of Disassociation

Most people don't realize they can fail and not be a failure. They have not learned to separate their worth as a person from their performance. These people find it difficult to have their ideas, work or accomplishments criticized. They feel you are criticizing and rejecting who they are, not just what they did.

A teacher told one mother that her son was not a good student; he couldn't learn and would never amount to much. He was a failure. But the mother chose to believe in her son, rather than listen to the voice of this authority. As a result, that young man grew up in a home of loving acceptance, secure with the knowledge that he was a person of value. In spite of this, he continued to fail. In fact, he failed ten thousand times on the same project before he, Thomas Alva Edison, perfected the electric light bulb. It was his close association with failure that caused Edison to comment, "I failed my way to success"; but his mother's belief in him was the human fuel for his inventive spirit.

How can you help your mate learn to fail without feeling like a failure? Try not to discuss a problem in your marriage or family with accusing words such as, "you never (or always) . . ." or "your ideas are always (or never). . ." Those kinds of statements verbally link your mate with his performance, insinuating he is a failure. Instead, use your words with discernment to help him see the distinction between his personhood and his performance.

When discussing issues, begin by expressing your commitment and loyalty to him as a person. Then give your mate the benefit of the doubt. Remove the accusing edge by saying, "I may be wrong, but did you . . . " or "I feel that . . ." or "It would help me a lot if you would . . . (fill the car with gas, balance the checkbook, pick up your socks, etc.)."

You may find that your mate struggles with admitting he's failed. This may be largely due to the fact that too much of his self-worth is dependent upon his performance. By admitting failure, he would admit he doesn't have it all together, and an insecure person has difficulty admitting that. It's just too threatening. But don't give up. With time, he'll understand the difference between his worth as a person and the worth of performance.

Tell him the truth — he is loved by you, esteemed and valued by God, gifted, and yet limited. Call to mind his past accomplishments, but most important, help your mate separate himself from his failures. Focus on him as a *person*, too, not just on his successful performance. It is when your mate knows how to handle failure without *being* a failure that he truly has the freedom to fail.

 The Gift of Encouraging Decisive Living

Many times in life we fail not because we make the wrong decision, but because we make no decision at all. Seeking safety and security, we escape to the seemingly trouble-free world of procrastination and indecision. Never venturing out of our protective covering of indecision, we seek to avoid risking a wrong decision that might end in failure. We decide not to decide.

You can strengthen your mate by helping him see that a risk-free life is also a potentially boring and selfish life. By eliminating risk, we eliminate many pleasures, too. Security and safety are not found in hiding from reality and responsibility. In fact, quite the opposite is true. Failure ultimately looms on the horizon for the person who avoids the decision-making process. He is riding a fence with both feet firmly planted in mid-air — there is little stability.

If your mate tends to be overly dependent upon you for decisions, gently begin to push a few of them back to him. Sometimes verbalizing "You decide. I trust you. And I'll back you in whatever you decide" can be very freeing. In this way he learns he can make good decisions. Good decisions sprout self-confidence and increased trust in his own decision-making abilities.

 The Gift of Forgiveness

The effects of failure can be disarmed through the miracle of forgiveness. Forgive your mate when his error has affected you. Urge him to receive God's forgiveness and to forgive himself, if necessary. The act of forgiveness opens the door to healing.

Paul again has some good advice: "And be kind to one another, tender-hearted, forgiving each other, just as God in Christ also has forgiven you."[7] And "Bearing with one another, and forgiving each other, whoever has a complaint against any one, just as the Lord forgave you, so also should you."[8]

Perhaps your mate's failure caused you to be late, which you hate. Maybe his failure cost him a bonus which you were counting on to be able to buy that new loveseat. Because of your partnership in marriage, your mate's mistakes and failures will affect you to some degree. Whatever the situation, mistakes carry a price tag. It can be extra work, suffering, financial expense — or all three. (All failures need the balm of forgiveness.) When you forgive, you give up your right to punish. It's an act of the will — a deliberate choice that means you will not retaliate when you feel the other person has wronged you. True forgiveness doesn't throw your mate's failures back at him or use them to hurt him.

Beware, too, of rationalization. Don't say to yourself, "My wife is more at fault in this than I am, so I'll be doggoned if I'm going to give in and ask to be forgiven." That's pride talking. Keep in mind that people seldom evaluate situations with an unbiased view. As the old line goes, "Rare is the person who can weigh the faults of others without putting his thumb on the scale."

The gift of forgiveness is not just *giving* forgiveness, but *asking* for it when you're wrong. Whether you're 90 percent in the wrong, or only 10 percent, asking forgiveness takes the logs out of the fire. Verbalize it. Be specific. And don't fudge. Some people try to weasel out of their responsibility so as never to admit they were wrong. But in doing so, they miss the benefits of forgiveness.

Pure and free, forgiveness gives us something we often don't deserve. This is how God relates to us as His children. He has given us love when we deserved punishment. Forgiveness says, "I won't reject you for your failures. I choose to accept you fully, just as you are and I won't remind you of your failures."

Forgiveness stands with the open arms of a loving relationship, ready to embrace. It is illogical for your mate to resist such an aggressive love. By removing the fear of rejection, you give your mate renewed hope to keep trying without fear of failure.

Give Him the Freedom to Fail

The solution, therefore, is not to seek to fill your lives only with successes, nor is it just to avoid failure. That is impossible, anyway. Instead, give each other the freedom to fail, and support one another when you do fail.

Two people together can be like suspenders; when one falls, there's always the assurance of the other holding on. You and your mate need each other to help build the self-worth that comes from inside. And when your mate fails by sinning, he needs you to point him back to Christ, who always stands ready to receive and accept us.

By gaining a perspective on failure and how it affects your mate, you will be better at loving, nurturing and caring for him. More important, understanding your mate's response to risk and failure can aid you in building his self-esteem.

ESTEEM BUILDER PROJECT
(Use a sheet of paper if necessary.)

1. Evaluate your mate's "fear factor." How fearful is he? A little? A lot? Only occasionally? Frequently?
2. List in order of priority the two or three "gifts" from this chapter that you need to give to your mate. Write beside

each gift how you will reinforce its truth practically in your mate's life.

The Gift of Compassion _____

_____

The Gift of Affirmation _____

_____

The Gift of Perspective _____

_____

The Gift of Disassociation _____

_____

The Gift of Encouraging Decisive Living _____

_____

The Gift of Forgiveness _____

_____

3. Why not give your mate authorized freedom to fail? You can formally present him with a document to that effect, custom designed and signed by you and notarized to make it official.

Pleasing Your Mate

By focusing on pleasing your mate, you communicate that he is valued, cherished and loved.

— 10 —
New Furnishings for an Empty Home

- A Special Classified Ad
- Pleasing Your Mate Produces Value
- Why Don't We Please?
- "Pass the Poison, Please"
- Reality Overtakes Romance
- Familiarity Breeds Complacency
- Fear, Neglect, and Bitterness
- Requirements of a Partner Pleaser
- Pleasing Your Mate Requires Accurate Knowledge
- A Partner Pleaser Is Sacrificial
- A Partner Pleaser Is Adventuresome
- Ideas for Pleasing
- Benefits of Pleasing Your Mate
- Be a Grateful Receiver
- Esteem Builder Project

Building Block 6: Pleasing Your Mate

A CLASSIFIED AD read as follows:

For Sale: One 52-year-old husband. Never remembers anniversaries, birthdays, or special days. Seldom holds hands, hugs, kisses, or says, "I love you." Rarely is kind or tender. Will sell cheap — two cents. Call 555-0366. Will dicker."

That advertisement illustrates the end result of a hollow marriage, one void of pleasing one another. Undoubtedly that woman's self-worth bore the mark of her husband's lack of attention. Had her husband made a conscious effort to strengthen her self-worth by pleasing her, that advertisement never would have appeared.

139

Did this husband begin their courtship and marriage with this list of "nevers"? It's doubtful. This couple, as most young couples, probably experienced the pleasure and delight of pleasing one another, for the desire to please is born out of love. But why is pleasing one another so bountiful in courtship and engagement and in the spring of marriage, but so scarce in the other seasons of a maturing marriage?

Before we answer that question, let's explore how pleasing your mate builds his self-esteem.

Pleasing Your Mate Produces Value

To please means "to satisfy, make content, gratify, gladden, cheer, delight." When we are pleased, we smile. Our smile indicates happiness and satisfaction.

Just as new upholstery changes an old worn chair into a piece of furniture that looks brand new, so pleasing your mate can refurbish his self-esteem. When you pay attention to what pleases your mate, you validate his uniqueness as a person. Knowing his interests and acting to accommodate them lets him know you care. Whether it's fixing the screen door, spicing up your sex life, carrying out a promise, losing fifteen pounds, working more around the house, or being on time, your actions communicate, "You're number one, and I want you to know it."

What could you do right now to please your mate? What would cause his face to beam with excitement? Do you know? Will you do it? When? If not, why not? If you really love him, why wouldn't you want to please him all the time?

Why Don't We Please?

Isn't it fascinating that during the courtship phase, men and women compete vigorously for the prize of marriage, and when the "right one" is found, both members of the relationship apply the pleasing principle to its maximum? They jog and work out for one another. Young women spend hours maintaining the best image, and they attend all kinds of sporting events, regardless of whether they enjoy them or even understand the game. As the popular song of the late '60s says:

". . . Do the things he likes to do,
wear your hair just for him, 'cause
you won't get him thinkin' and a-prayin',
wishin' and a-hopin'. . ."[1]

Men are no different. A young man will take the time for picnics and walks in the park. He may save his meager earnings for flowers, cards, letters and gifts. He's so thoughtful. He treats her to evenings on the town. She feels like a queen, proud to be with such a considerate man. They talk for hours and dream of the future. Confidence grows that this blissful state will last forever.

Then the wedding ceremony comes and goes. Almost overnight, couples are transformed into tightwad pragmatists. They've "won the prize." But the desire to please, which so recently flowed instinctively, begins to recede like a desert stream as the summer heat intensifies. Familiarity has stolen initiative, and the challenge is apparently over. Finally, pleasing virtually stops. What started as a dream fades away as disillusionment replaces romance. The life cycle of pleasing has abruptly ended.

"Pass the Poison, Please"

One of the most bitter relationships recorded in this generation, one full of sarcasm, was between two of Britain's finest individuals: Sir Winston Churchill and Lady Astor. Although not married to each other, these two typify what happens to far too many husbands and wives.

On one occasion she intended to insult him when she said, "Mr. Churchill, if you were my husband, I'd give you poison to drink."

His quick reply shot back, "Lady, if you were my wife, I'd drink it."

But Lady Astor didn't give up easily. On another occasion she saw her golden opportunity, for Churchill had been drinking liberally. Lady Astor, probably assuming he would not have the presence of mind to retaliate, accused him indignantly, saying, "Mr. Prime Minister, I perceive you are drunk."

A wry smile broke across Churchill's face as he retorted with, "Yes, Lady, and I perceive you are ugly. But tomorrow I shall be sober."

As in Churchill's and Astor's relationship, many marriage partners today have traded pleasing one another for poisoning one another. They have swapped positive words for negative, piercing ones.

Reality Overtakes Romance

Why do so many couples stop pleasing one another? Because reality replaces romance. Any couple can handle romance; it's like falling off a cliff together. Who hasn't enjoyed being under the influence of romance's gravity? But then they hit the ground. Suddenly, paying bills and saving for the future leaves little money for flowers. Jobs must be done, meals must be cooked, and babies must be held and fed, so no time remains for walks in the park. They become so busy surviving or striving for that lifestyle that they don't have the creative energy to consider how to please their mates. "Besides," they tell themselves, "He knows I love him," or "She knows I care."

Familiarity Breeds Complacency

With romantic feelings waning, familiarity and complacency can move into marriage. We become content with the status quo; there is not much more to learn about the other person. Duty replaces desire as the motivational force in pleasing your mate. It's not that serving him out of obligation is wrong, but the spirit in which it's done makes pleasing him either a joy or a chore. Your mate will sense the difference, and will feel valued or unimportant, depending on your motivation.

Fear Fuels Self-Protection

Without the fire of those strong feelings warming you and giving you courage, the chill of fear makes you introspective and cautious. Now you are hesitant to give, to share, to sacrifice. Slowly, you erect barriers to protect yourself. You seek to meet your own needs rather than give to your mate. Instead of allowing you to reach out and take a risk, your fear tells you to play it safe. You resist venturing into areas that are unfamiliar or that represent a threat to your security. So your mate feels alone and isolated, and his self-esteem begins to erode.

Neglect Is Dangerous

When a spouse feels neglected and bored at home, he or she may seek excitement elsewhere. One of the chief ingredients in extra-marital affairs is the fresh interest that two people express in each another. Consequently, both become good listeners, and the competition is on again.

Too often people ignore those closest to them. With the "prize" secured, they don't think of maintaining the strength of their relationships in order to keep the competition at bay. Frequently they neglect their mates because they are selfish and it's the easiest thing to do. But they *are* still competing for their mates, or at least they should be. If they do not focus on their mates, they leave the door wide open for others to come in and look around. They lose by default.

In a healthy way, we try to stay mindful that the competition is not over. Yes, we are secure. But, no, we are not lazy. And we realize men and women will not go shopping for pleasure, fulfillment, excitement or companionship if they have all they can handle at home.

Have you neglected your mate? Why not start competing for him again? Done in a healthy manner, it's fun.

Remove Any Bitterness

Perhaps you aren't interested in pleasing your mate because you are angry at him and want to punish him. People who are embittered against their partners don't realize they are harming themselves as much as their mates, or more so. As someone has said, a marital conflict is like a shoot-out between Siamese twins!

Possibly you're bitter because you have tried to please your mate, only to find you've fallen short of his expectations. You may have decided that pleasing your mate is an impossible task. Why not ask forgiveness for your bitterness, and try to please him again, and again, and again...no matter how he responds? (For more information on this, refer to chapter 9.)

REQUIREMENTS OF A PARTNER PLEASER

1. Pleasing your mate requires accurate knowledge.

The best way to find out how to please your mate is to ask, "What could I do to please you? What three things really please you? What things, if I do them, will communicate love, worth and value from me to you?"

Too often we fall into the trap of confusing what pleases our mate with what pleases us. Only recently Barbara pointed this out to me (Dennis). As a sign of my affection, I was gently rubbing the back of Barbara's neck. She looked up at me and smiled, "We've been married fourteen years. When do you think you'll remember that I don't like having my neck rubbed?"

Since I like having my neck and back rubbed, I automatically think Barbara does, too. Yet for more than fourteen years, Barbara has told me she does not like it. Maybe someday I will learn!

Another route toward gathering knowledge is observation and listening. Has your mate ever said, "I really like . . ." or "I wish sometime you would . . ."? If so, that is the place to start your efforts in pleasing him. Observe him. Where does he experience repeated frustrations? Can you help there? Are you willing?

To keep the communication lines open and to remain informed about each other's lives, try to establish a regular time together for planning, talking and dreaming. We *try* to set aside Sunday evenings as our time to talk and think through our calendars and schedules. When will we spend special time with the children? When will we spend special time together? Planning communicates we care enough to consult one another ahead of time. It instills value. And consistently spending that time talking together increases our knowledge of each other and provides opportunities to please.

2. *A partner pleaser is sacrificial.*

In our economy, one usually determines the value of a piece of merchandise or a service by how much one has to give up, or sacrifice, to gain it. If my son wishes to buy a leather basketball, it will cost him three weekends of freedom to earn the money to pay for it. Therefore, the value Benjamin places on the ball is three weekends.

In a similar fashion, your mate often interprets how much you love or value him by what you are willing to sacrifice.

Some sacrifices are easily recognizable. These include special gifts on standard occasions and for no reason at all. You need not always give large gifts, but don't fall into the rut of always giving small or inexpensive ones either. And remember, surprises are fun at any age. They bring pleasure and they help your mate feel special. That, in turn, helps build his self-esteem.

As a man, I doubt if I will ever understand why women get so excited about flowers. But I do realize I don't need to understand "why." I just need to know that I periodically should give them to Barbara. A bouquet of flowers is a small sacrifice that carries a large value and says, "I love you."

For the woman who is trying to please her husband, it often has been said that the way to a man's heart is through his stomach. Why not cook the foods he enjoys? Be careful not to become his mother, feeding him only what is "good for him." Spoil him a little. This says you care enough to sacrifice your standards to please him. And men, take your wives out to a special dinner, even when it's *not* her birthday.

Another form of sacrifice in marriage comes when we show an interest in our mate's hobbies and pastimes. I (Barbara) have always had an interest in art and enjoy looking at paintings in art galleries and museums. When we married, Dennis had no such interest. He considered art museums a great place to get bored quickly. But to please me, Dennis has gone to quite a few museums. He also encouraged me to take watercolor lessons. He even asks questions to learn more about this part of me. The other night, he disregarded the evening newscast to look through an art catalog with me. It wasn't a big sacrifice, but it communicated a respect that made me feel valued. His involvement told me, "I care about the things you enjoy."

In contrast, though Dennis has always loved fishing, I had no appreciation for the sport. I tended to agree with the person who said, "A fisherman is a jerk on one end waiting for a jerk on the other." Fishing seemed a boring waste of time. But to please Dennis, I did a lot of fishing in the early years of our marriage. Later, when our growing population of children made it impossible for me to go, I encouraged him to go alone or with some other men.

In the process of pleasing each other, we each have become richer. Our horizons have been expanded. I have learned there is skill, patience, perseverance and reward in fishing. I no longer see it as a waste of time. Fishing has become important to me, because it's part of what makes Dennis who he is. We have great vacation memories of going fishing at night while our children were asleep.

On the other hand, Dennis has developed a growing interest in art. He even enjoys museums (in regulated doses). The detail and depth of classical painting and sculpture now produce in him amazement and respect — not sleep.

The final form of sacrifice we wish to discuss is probably

the most important: time. You can make more money, and you
can buy more flowers, but you can't make or buy more time.
Each day has twenty-four hours — nothing will change that.
You have 86,400 seconds in a day. How will you spend them?
If you sleep for eight hours and work for nine hours, you
have only 25,200 seconds left. What is their best use?

How often do you hear, "I'd love to, but I don't have
enough time"; or "Sure, let's get together, *if* we can find the
time"; and "What am I going to do? I'm running out of time!"?
We're all running out of time. Psalm 90:12 admonishes us to
"number our days." How many do you have left? How will
you use them?

To give your time requires the greatest sacrifice. Does
your work deserve it? Or does your wife and family? Do you
want to communicate your love to your wife? If so, give her
your time . . . undivided, and focused on her. Take time for
a quiet walk or a scenic drive. Above all else, simply take
time for each other. If blood is the gift of life, then time is
the gift of love.

3. A partner pleaser is adventuresome.

Marriage was never intended to become boring. But unless
you work at adding adventure, your marriage can become dull,
filled only with the routines of life. Life is too short to waste.
Why not become a bit unpredictable and add some sizzle to
your mate and to your marriage? Your mate's self-image will
grow as you become an adventuresome partner.

All of us have been or will be called upon to express
love to our mate in a way that goes outside our comfort zone.
This is especially difficult if we value our comfort above
pleasing our mate. To venture beyond our comfort, trust must
be assured. No one wants to be vulnerable or to try to please
another and be laughed at or rejected. Let your mate know
that your efforts to please him might be a little shaky at first.
Tell him you need him to appreciate your beginning efforts.

One area in most marriages that tends to become predictable is sex. Find out what specifically pleases your mate, and
continue to communicate and grow in this intimate area of
your marriage relationship. Also, express what pleases you,
not just what doesn't. Almost every person derives great satisfaction out of pleasing someone he loves. But if the recipient
does not express appreciation in return, then the giver is left

to wonder if he pleased his mate.

Occasionally you may need to move out of your comfort zone and risk something new in the effort to please your mate. By being adventuresome, you will communicate love. On the other hand, an unwillingness to grow, risk and try something new can be a negative statement of value to your mate, as well as a point of resentment.

A wife needs to dress to please her husband (if it's important to him). She should remain attractive to him. She should be willing to splurge occasionally on lingerie and to put on a "little something special" without him having to ask.

A husband must provide plenty of romance and tenderness. He needs to continue to communicate love, affection and caring.

In the ebb and flow of life, needs and emotions change, requiring continued sensitivity by both mates. You cannot please your mate physically without risk, without first learning and being sensitive to his needs.

Keep in touch, literally. When you were dating, touching was as automatic as pleasing one another. In fact, it was a part of the expression of romance. For many married couples, touching is a forgotten avenue of communicating worth. Learn the delights of touching one another as you did when you were dating: Hold hands, embrace, stroll arm in arm, etc. Share with one another where you like to be touched and how. Nonsexual body touching can be a small but important way to communicate, "I want to give you a little bit of pleasure."

As you consider areas that would please your mate, but that are tough for you, stop and contemplate the alternative. Millions of marriages are dead because both partners have stopped trying to please one another. Tell your Heavenly Father how you feel and ask Him to give you the courage and the strength to try again. Then stir the sparks of creativity to life. Give, without demanding a response or even looking for one.

Benefits of Pleasing Your Mate

Pleasing your mate will not spoil him. It doesn't mean indulgence to the point of throwing common sense away. It doesn't mean you become a slave, dutifully obeying commands. You are a partner. You have the honored position of being your mate's lover. And being a lover is far more than being a sexual partner. It's loving the total person. It's respecting him and

IDEAS FOR PLEASING

For the creative, pleasing your mate may be a natural part of your personality. But those less creative may need some coaching tips for becoming a partner pleaser. And all of us

---

THINGS FOR A MAN TO DO TO PLEASE HIS WIFE:
1. Take the children out for a few hours.
2. Take her on a picnic that you have put together.
3. Fix the leaky faucet.
4. Rake the yard and plant some bushes or flowers, etc.
5. Leave her a love note . . . under the pillow, in her purse, pocket, etc.
6. Make all the arrangements for an evening out, i.e., call the babysitter, make dinner reservations, and possibly stay overnight in a hotel.
7. Send her a card for no reason at all — maybe one that reminds you both of a special memory.
8. Have a scavenger hunt with the final reward being a special gift or a trip for two.
9. Use the phone. Call her just to say, "I love you and was thinking about you."
10. Do one thing you did when you first met and were dating.

---

being glad he is the way he is. If you love him, you will want to please him. Jesus equated love with action, when He said, "He who has My commandments and keeps them, he it is who loves Me."[2]

Romans 15:2,3a says, "Let each of us please his neighbor for his good, to his edification. For even Christ did not please Himself." Who is your closest neighbor? Your mate. How can you edify (build, improve) your mate and thereby enhance his self-worth? By discovering — and doing — what pleases him.

Pleasing your mate is a preservative in your marriage, as salt is in foods. It brings out the flavor of your unique relationship. It brings delight to your mate. His self-esteem is built because you make him feel valuable, special, important.

need an occasional cue card to remind us to reach out. We are including on these pages some lists of common partner pleasers. Pick something you haven't tried before; don't give complacency a foothold.

THINGS FOR A WOMAN TO DO TO PLEASE HER HUSBAND:

1. Write him a letter and send it to his office or put a love note in his lunch box, briefcase, etc.
2. Prepare his favorite meal.
3. Arrange for an evening out for just the two of you.
4. Wear his favorite dress with your hair done the way he likes it.
5. Wear his favorite negligée.
6. Purchase something small and frivolous for him that he won't buy himself.
7. Give him a nicely framed picture of you or you and the children for his office.
8. Surprise him with an all-expense-paid overnight golf, fishing, or hunting trip.
9. Put the children to bed early and prepare a candlelight dinner.
10. Do something that especially pleased him when you were dating.

And the enchantment and thrill of first love will return to you, giving your own worth an extra boost.

Be a Grateful Receiver

If, as a result of reading this chapter, your mate begins to take risks and to do things to please you, be sure you are a grateful receiver. Being appreciative is the best way to insure the giving will continue. Putting down or not noticing the first steps of pleasing will quench the tiny flame of giving love. So express approval and gratitude. Praise your mate, even if his attempts to please you end in a failure the first time around. Build him up and you will likely receive again.

Remember, learning to please your mate requires time.

ESTEEM BUILDER PROJECT
(Use a sheet of paper if necessary.)

1. What truly pleases your mate? List in order of priority five things you could do that would please him.
2. Why not consider doing the one thing that would please your mate most today or this weekend? Set a time on your calendar to do it, and then follow through.

Doing What Is Right

Your genuine applause for right choices will motivate
your mate toward an obedient lifestyle.

— 11 —
Turning Cheap Imitations
Into Priceless Originals

- The Heart of Self-Worth Is Our Relationship With God
- Are You Faking the Christian Life?
- Pleasing God Is Satisfying
- Eli's Sons Chose Disobedience Toward God
- How to Encourage Obedient Living (and Thereby Build Self-Esteem)
- Dennis Exposes His Own Charade
- Model Obedience to Christ
- Applaud Right Choices
- Tips for Encouraging Obedience
- Pray for Obedience
- Esteem Builder Project

Building Block 7: Doing What Is Right

HAVE YOU EVER "faked" the Christian life? Or have you watched your mate "act religious" when you knew he was far from God? Can you recall how you feel when you disobey God and what it is like for your mate to live with you when you are ignoring a command of Scripture?

At the heart of self-worth is our relationship with God. Our obedience to Him secures a sense of well-being and contentment. He gives us peace when we are faithful, when we "hear" His Word and "do it."[1]

On the other hand, our disobedience can result in a heavy yoke of guilt. Knowing that God's displeasure or anger is burning against us, we cannot experience a positive self-worth. We feel as valuable as a counterfeit $100 bill.

Some people are pretty good counterfeits — excellent fakes. Their lives may have all the appearances of Christianity. Publicly they may do an abundance of "Christian deeds" and use the right Christian clichés, but privately their lives are a charade. They aren't listening to God. Their lives are a mockery.

A young man had just graduated from law school and had set up an office, proudly displaying his shingle out front. On his first day at work, as he sat at his desk with his door open, he wondered how to get his first client. Then he heard footsteps coming down the long corridor toward his office.

Not wanting this potential client to think he would be his first, he quickly picked up the telephone and began to talk loudly to a make-believe caller.

"Oh, yes sir," the young lawyer exclaimed into the phone, "I'm very experienced in corporate law. . . . Courtroom experience? Why, yes, I've had several cases."

The sound of steps drew closer to his open door.

"I have broad experience in almost every category of legal work," he continued, loud enough for his impending visitor to hear.

Finally, with the steps right at his door, he replied, "Expensive? Oh, no sir, I'm very reasonable. I'm told my rates are among the lowest in town."

The young lawyer then excused himself from his "conversation" and covered the phone to respond to the prospective client who was now standing in the doorway. With his most confident voice he said, "Yes, sir, may I help you?"

"Well, yes you can," the man said with a smirk. "I'm the telephone repairman, and I've come to hook up your phone!"

We sometimes fake the Christian life in this same way. Preoccupied with self and wanting our own way, we ignore God and pretend to be spiritual. Instead of having Christ's character imprinted on our lives, we go our own way, and our Christianity becomes a forgery. Like that counterfeit $100 bill, we may look real, but we lack genuine value.

Pleasing God Is Satisfying

The basis of obedience is faith. Living by faith is not passive — it requires action. We listen to God's Word and then obey, putting shoe leather to His commands. We please God when we walk by faith. "And without faith it is impossible to please Him, for he who comes to God must believe that He is, and that He is a rewarder of those who seek Him."[2]

Just as obedience is a choice, so is disobedience. It's a refusal to listen, a rejection of the truth. We say by our actions that we don't believe that what God says is reliable or accurate.

When we willfully disobey God, we lose our peaceful feelings of value, and we do not experience His love and forgiveness. This does *not* mean we are worth any less in God's eyes. We only experience *feelings* of worthlessness. God's love for even the most rebellious Christian never diminishes. (Take a look at the promise of Romans 8:31-39 and the story of the prodigal son in Luke 15:11-32.) But the inner sense of our priceless worth as Christians fades when we live in either passive or willful disobedience before God.

Eli's Boys

The Scriptures include many stories of those who fell under God's disapproval because of disobedience. One of the most tragic is the account of Eli's family. We are told in 1 Samuel about this father and his two sons who were in the priesthood of the nation of Israel. Their inherited responsibility was to give spiritual leadership to the people. However, Eli's sons were not interested in serving God. "Now the sons of Eli were *worthless* men; they did not know the Lord" (italics added).[3]

Not only did they not know God, but they also didn't even care enough to observe the customs of the priesthood. These men abused their role as priests. "Thus the sin of the young men was very great before the Lord, for the men *despised* the offering of the Lord" (italics added).[4] The word *despise* means "to scorn, feel disgust toward, hate, loathe, abhor, laugh at." These are strong words. They tell us how the sons of Eli felt about God and His prescribed plan for man (the offerings). The sons chose disobedience and their lifestyle was flagrantly rebellious.

Notice what God said to Eli several verses later: "Those who honor [revere, respect, value, esteem] Me I will honor, and those who despise Me will be *lightly esteemed*."[5]

HOW TO ENCOURAGE OBEDIENT LIVING
(And Thereby Build Self-Esteem)

If obedience to God is necessary for a positive self-image, and if obedience is essentially an individual matter, then how can you use this building block to shape your mate's self-esteem? You can't obey for him, can you? No; although at times you may wish you could, he must make his own choices.

So how can you help your mate obey God? There are several things you can do, but first, you must meet a prerequisite in your own life.

Dennis Exposes His Own Charade

For more than thirteen years, I faked it in church. Oh, I had my moments of feeling close to God, when I saw a beautiful sunset or did something good "for the Lord." I was a Christian, but for the most part, I was "playing church." My Christian life consisted of little more than "fire insurance" and making a once-a-week trip to the "agent's office."

I was going my own way. I chose either to ignore God's prescribed path for my life, or to flagrantly disobey it. I was going to run my own show and didn't see why God should have any meaningful part in it.

My life was a living example of a statement made by John Calvin, the great reformation leader. He said, "The torture of a bad conscience is the hell of a living soul."

When I turned twenty, however, something happened. I had accomplished every goal I had set at that point in my life. I was prospering. Everything I touched seemed to turn to "gold," yet I still didn't feel good about myself. The fulfillment that came with these accomplishments was fleeting. I was empty and lacking self-respect and value. I knew I was compromising what God had commanded. I was doing my best to ignore Jesus Christ on a daily basis.

Ultimately my emptiness drove me back to my Christian roots to find the forgiveness and the God I felt I needed. Through a friend's guidance, I began to study the Bible and found that God loved me and wanted His best for me. I discovered there was no comparison between God's best for my life and my own "best." I was living in a fuzzy, two-dimensional, black-and-white world, while by comparison God had a crystal-clear, full-color, three-dimensional experience waiting for me . . . if I would only obey Him.

I came to the conclusion that I had been treating Jesus Christ like a spare tire. When I got in trouble, I'd pull Him out of the trunk for a couple of days, but then stick Him back in the trunk until I had another flat. It dawned on me that the God of the universe who loved me so much did not come to be a spare tire, a hitchhiker, or just my driving companion. Christ came to be Lord of my life; the owner and driver of my life.

I recall being astonished that the God of creation valued me so highly; that He still called me His son even though I had not called Him "Father" for years. His relentless love just kept coming after me.

Finally, I gave in. And I gave up. I relinquished all rights of my life to Him and, over a period of three months, my life was placed back in His hands. Instead of treating Him as a spare tire and a hitchhiker, I gave Him ownership of my life and let Him take over the steering wheel.

By submitting to His plan for my life, I'm convinced the life I now live is more valuable and exciting than anything I could possibly have had by going my own way. Walking with God and obeying Him on a daily basis provides a sense of worth and value that is beyond description. I have peace of mind from pleasing the living Lord of the universe. I can't imagine living any other way.

Giving God the Lordship — allowing God's daily control — is fundamental to self-image and a prerequisite to obedience. Once a life is submitted to Christ, thousands of decisions lie ahead, which will either validate that commitment or prove it wrong. But thankfully, the choices come one at a time. Those daily forks in the road, added together, can produce a self-esteem of value and worth.

Once you are yielded to Jesus Christ by faith, allowing His power to work in and through your life, then you can spur your mate on to becoming an obedient Christian, and in doing so elevate his self-worth. Here are some ways.

1. Model obedience.

The best way to encourage your mate to yield to Christ is to model a life of obedience to Him. A model is an example. Models are used in many professions, including medicine and dentistry, and in most fields of art. They are used in architecture and science as illustrations. They also are studied and observed carefully for the purpose of copying or gaining more knowledge.

In the same way, in your marriage you are a model to your mate. Your life is under observation by the one closest to you. It's unavoidable.

Does your life demonstrate obedience? Do you live what you believe or merely talk it? What knowledge does your mate gain about godliness, contentment and prayer from your example (not your words)? Would your mate want to copy the model you exhibit?

Jesus referred to His disciples as the salt and light of the world.[6] Your assignment is to create an environment where your mate can see (light) what the Christian life really is and can become thirsty (salt) for that lifestyle himself.

Become an example by walking and fellowshiping with God (not to be confused with church "work"), as well as by yielding your life to Him by faith. You will become salt and light to your mate as your life evidences the peace and contentment God promises.

Modeling obedience to Christ is impossible unless you are filled with the Holy Spirit. As you surrender daily by faith to His power, you grow and mature as a Christian. Therefore, continue to submit to the Scriptures, and the Holy Spirit in you will become the model your mate needs to see.

2. Applaud right choices.

Your mate needs you to be a cheerleader, not a preacher. Praise and applaud your mate's right choices. It will encourage him to trust God again. Don't just tell him what he doesn't do right. Most likely he aleady receives daily reminders from a host of others.

One couple faced losing their home because of a mistake made in preparing their income tax. The amount owed was a sizable one, and it seemed entirely possible that the only way they could pay the debt was by selling their home.

There was another option, however. As they discussed their situation over the next three days, they were given all sorts of advice from attorneys and tax consultants. Not all of the advice was ethical. They were told there was a strong possibility the IRS would never find out. The error might never be detected. They were tempted to wait it out.

Yet, they knew what they had to do. The choice was clear, but not easy. The wife urged her husband to do the right thing. She told him, "I want you to do what's right, even if it means selling the house."

And they did what was right. They decided to file an amended return and pay the balance owed, even if the house had to be sold. It was an agonizing decision, for they had worked hard on their home to make it just the way they wanted it.

After making the decision, they looked at each other and swallowed hard. But inside they had a firm assurance that their choice was pleasing to God. Their confidence seemed to grow with each passing moment.

Some days later, with smiles on their faces they shared how they had worked through their temptation. Because of their right decision, they had peace with God, and another brick was laid firmly in place in their character and self-image. They learned the truth of what Francis Bacon said: "A good conscience is a continual feast." And, in the end, they didn't have to sell their home.

We, too, have faced many temptations in our marriage. We have been tempted to be unfaithful, to take the other for granted, to say something that would wound deeply, or to become embittered toward the other over a matter of disagreement.

But in each of these and others, we have worked on verbalizing to each other our temptations. We tell each other how we feel. Then we talk about a solution.

In each situation, appreciation is expressed to the one for sharing that problem and to the other for responding positively. We applaud the transparency and truthfulness of the one being tempted. We do not sermonize the truth, but instead affirm the person and encourage him or her to do what is right. The result has been great freedom and great trust in our marriage.

Likewise, you can support your mate for doing what's right. Cheer his right choices. Affirm him. Tell your mate you admire him when he stands for what is right and that it inspires you to follow Christ, too.

And if your mate goes off in the wrong direction, hang in there with him. Pray for him. Love him intensely.

Another way to encourage obedience in your mate is to express verbal appreciation for his convictions and character. Convictions and character are shaped when we cooperate with God's Spirit and obey His truth.

TIPS FOR ENCOURAGING OBEDIENCE

Here are some tips that we've found helpful in our marriage when one of us wants to do "his own thing":

1. Don't nag. Love him for who he is. Being nagged is like being nibbled to death by a duck.
2. Don't plot. Instead, pray for her.
3. Don't look for him to obey God perfectly every time.
4. Don't tear her down for who she isn't and what she doesn't do. Build her up, even when you think she doesn't deserve it.
5. Don't listen to ungodly counsel that tells you to quit. Surround yourself with Christians who will encourage you to fulfill your marriage vows.
6. Pray for your mate to be surrounded by godly Christians who will love him and share with him what he needs to hear. (Don't do it yourself. Let God.)

Do you frequently tell your mate you are proud of him for what he stands for? For his good reputation in the community? For his consistently making right choices and the example he is to your family? By praising and elevating your mate's character, you reinforce values that are close to God's heart.

3. Pray for obedience.

Building you mate's self-image requires a partnership between you and God. No one can do it alone. The importance of prayer for your mate cannot be underestimated.

"The effective prayer of a righteous man can accomplish much."[7] Effective prayer is asking God to do what He already wants to do in your mate's life. God delights in answering such prayer, for He wants you to know Him, to see Him work, and to continue to come to Him.

Praying for your mate over a lifetime together is a privilege few people have. The Scriptures tell us, "You do not have because you do not ask."[8] We need to go to God repeatedly with our needs and requests, expecting Him to act on our behalf. Paul admonishes us, "Pray without ceasing."[9]

Be careful of praying negatively for that list of things

you don't like in your mate. Instead, pray positively. View your prayers as an opportunity to team up with God in building godly qualities into your mate. Come before God's throne on his behalf requesting that he will know God's love more fully; that God will develop a teachable, pure heart within him. Pray for an increased desire to obey and follow Christ. Ask God to give him a growing awareness of the benefits of walking with Him. Ask too for faithfulness, contentment, patience, self-control, discipline and other godly values to be developed in his life. Study the Scriptures (start with 1 Corinthians 13; Romans 12; and Galatians 5:22,23) and ask God what else to include in your prayers.

Years ago we received a phone call from a woman who was desperate. Her husband was not interested in spiritual things and she had done everything she could think of to make it "reasonable" for him to make a commitment. Christian books were left open by his side of the bed, with portions underlined in bright ink. Tracts and pamphlets were scattered all around the house. It probably resembled a well-stocked Christian bookstore.

Tapes were left in the cassette player in his car, turned to just the right place. And if he pulled out the cassette, guess what station she had the radio tuned to? The local Christian broadcast. That button on his radio was pre-set to get "the word" to him. Poor fellow.

After talking for some time, she finally listened as we gave her our advice: "Don't say another word to your husband about Christ — no books, tapes, notes, tracts, and no more setting up meetings for other couples to corner him. Just live the Christian life and *pray*. If he asks a question about your faith, you can answer. Just obey Christ and pray for your husband. But don't say another word — not even one!"

Up to that point, this woman had concluded that God couldn't do it without her. She was doing God a favor by staying after her husband! But reluctantly, she agreed to follow our advice. She applied the principle found in 1 Peter 3:1-6, and she began the process of winning her husband "without a word."

Not much happened for the first few months, yet she remained silent. Then God's Word and her speechless strategy began to work. Slowly her husband warmed up to spiritual things. A year or so later, he started going to a Bible study with a group of businessmen. And a few months after that, he received Christ and became a growing Christian and witness for Him.

We wish we could promise you and every reader of this book that this woman's answered prayer would be a reality in your marriage as well. Unfortunately, there is no such promise, but don't give up. No matter what your situation, there is hope. *Your* life and *your* prayers are the key.

God Is Bigger Than Your Mate

Do you believe that God is bigger than your mate? Do you believe that God is fully capable of getting his attention? Does He have to use *you* to get your spouse's heart turned toward Him?

Sometimes we forget that God loves our mates more than we do, that He desires that our spouses be totally yielded to Him.

As Christians, we have little appreciation for God's power. We live as though He were some weak and senile old man who needs our help to get His work done. This is true especially in our thinking about our mates. We feel that only we can possibly straighten out our spouses.

In thinking this, we have taken God's place. Yet only God, the Good Shepherd, knows and can employ the most effective methods for getting the attention of a wayward sheep. Just ask Him to do so, and He will in His timing. Assist God in the right way, by modeling and applauding obedience and by praying.

Confidence Through Submission

Unfortunately, at times we all choose the wrong fork in the road. We don't do what's right. When this is true of your mate, don't be a "finger-pointer." Remember the lessons on failure and give your mate the space and freedom to fail.

Abraham knew the satisfaction of a life lived obediently before God. It's recorded in Genesis 25:8: "And Abraham breathed his last and died . . . satisfied with life." He didn't die full of regrets. He died with the peacefulness that can come only as God's child walks in the power of God's Spirit and obeys Him.

Since we were made in God's image, it stands to reason that when we fully submit our lives to His control, we begin to recapture the identity and confidence that was intended for man in the beginning.

In the book, *Beyond Personality,* C. S. Lewis writes of the identity that is found in self-denial and surrender to Christ:

> The more we get what we call "ourselves" out of the way and let Him take over, the more truly ourselves we become. . . . In that sense our real selves are all waiting for us in Him. It is no good trying to "be myself" without Him. . . . The more I resist Him and try to live on my own, the more I become dominated by my own heredity and upbringing and surroundings and natural desires. . . .I am not, in my natural state, nearly so much of a person as I like to believe: Most of what I call "me" can be very easily explained. It is when I turn to Christ, when I give myself up to His Personality, that I first begin to have a real personality of my own. . . .
>
> But there must be a real giving up of the self. You must throw it away "blindly" so to speak. Christ will indeed give you a real personality: but you must not go to Him for the sake of that. As long as your own personality is what you are bothering about, you are not going to Him at all. The very first step is to try to forget about the self altogether. . . . Lose your life and you will save it. Submit to death, death of your ambitions and favourite wishes every day and death of your body — in the end: Submit with every fibre of your being, and you will find eternal life. Keep back nothing. . . . Nothing in you that has not died will ever be raised from the dead. Look for yourself, and you will find in the long run only hatred, loneliness, despair, rage, ruin, and decay. But look for Christ and you will find Him, and with Him everything else thrown in.[10]

ESTEEM BUILDER PROJECT

(Use a sheet of paper if necessary.)

1. Read the following box and write out your own contract with God as a couple.
2. (Optional) List areas where you need to model the Christian life for your mate to observe, and ask God to help you be an excellent model.

OUR CONTRACT WITH GOD

After we were married, we wanted to symbolize together what both of us already had done separately. So, our first Christmas together, we made up a "Title Deed To Dennis and Barbara Rainey's Life."

That Christmas, before giving gifts to each other, we signed our contract with God, granting Him complete ownership of our lives, marriage, and family. Both of us felt great satisfaction that what we had done was pleasing to God and was right. We have never regretted that decision.

That document is filed safely in our safe-deposit box with all of our other valuable papers as a reminder of who has ultimate ownership and authority over our lives. It is a reminder that our lives are not our own.

If you haven't already done this, study Luke 14:25-35 together and write your own contractual document. Together, give God total rights to your lives and family.

If your mate isn't ready to sign, then why not make your own individual contract with God? You can sign it by yourself. Put it in a safe place with your other valuable documents.

Helping Your Mate Develop Friends

By encouraging your mate to develop close friendships, you enable others to affirm his value and
significance.

— 12 —
Friends:
Reflectors That Magnify

- Friends Who Make You Feel Comfortable
- A Friend: Someone Who Chooses to Like Your Mate
- Friendship: Spokes on the Wheel
- Friendships Are Necessary
- A Word to Husbands
- A Word to Wives
- Every Couple Needs a "Couple Friend"
- Dennis: How Friends Helped Me
- Esteem Builder Project

Building Block 8: Helping Your Mate Develop Friends

IT WAS CHRISTMAS DAY, 1984. The home video equipment and the 35mm camera were busy from early morning till nearly noon. The living room was littered with tissue, ribbon and dozens of foil wrappers from Hershey's Kisses that had met their intended destiny. Five children filled the room with delighted squeals and constant motion, as if they were battery-charged toys. We sat and watched, enjoyed and directed . . . and yawned.

No extended family came to help us celebrate that year because I (Barbara) was more than eight months pregnant and due in two weeks. I was too tired to prepare a big Christmas dinner, so we had an ordinary lunch and some cookies. Then we cleaned up our mess, and the two youngest and I retreated upstairs for an afternoon nap.

By evening, we all felt a little lonely. We had enjoyed our day with just us, but we wanted to share the holiday with someone else. Fortunately, some friends invited us to drop in. So after an early dinner, we gathered the children and some diapers and new toys, bundled up, and drove to town.

We were a motley crew. Our four-year-old, Rebecca, had on the pajamas she had received from her grandma and grandpa and unwrapped early that morning. The others wore assorted collections of old and new clothing. I had on what had become my daily maternity uniform: jeans and a red plaid flannel shirt, one of only two or three things that still fit. I decided to put on no makeup that day, and Dennis, also choosing to go grubby, was unshaven.

Our friends, who had had family and feasting all day, greeted us at the door in their holiday finery. Our kids darted in the door and disappeared with theirs for a time of show and tell. We four adults, accompanied by their two-year-old and our Deborah, then almost twenty months, made our way to the dining room. After sampling some delicious Christmas sweets, we had a wonderful time of fellowship and conversation.

Friends Make You Feel Comfortable

We were with friends. The fact that our dress and appearance didn't match theirs was irrelevant. We felt accepted for who we were and valued without having to perform. We left feeling happy and content because we had shared ourselves with others and were accepted.

George Santayana said, "One's friends are that part of the human race with which one can be human." That's how we felt that December 25th. We came as we were, without pretense, and received the love of friends.

A Friend: Someone Who Chooses to Like Your Mate

A friendship, like marriage, is a chosen relationship. A friend is someone who admires your mate, believes he is worth his time and energy, and has chosen him, from among the throngs of people, to get to know.

One of our children's books says simply, "A friend is someone who likes you." You can count on a committed friend to overlook the petty things others use to pick your mate apart.

Yet, a good friend will confront your mate with painful truths, too, when he most needs to hear them.

But my mate and I like each other — we don't need friends, you may be thinking. A couple with no friends outside the marriage, however, will be unable to achieve a healthy, balanced self-confidence.

Friendship: Spokes on the Wheel

Marriage is like the hub of a wheel. It is the point of strength, and as such, it should provide the assurance of total acceptance. Here we find a haven from others' rejection and disapproval.

But no marriage was meant to bear the total responsibility for building self-esteem in another. That would be an enormous weight to carry alone. Instead, both partners need to reach out from the hub and extend the spokes of friendship that strengthen them and expand their horizon. They need others outside the marriage who affirm their value and worth. These spokes, or friends, do not threaten the security and strength of the hub. Instead, the marriage is actually *enhanced* by the presence of a few stout and loyal friends.

Friendships Are Necessary

In a mature relationship, a man and a woman can acknowledge their deep needs to each other without insisting that those needs be met only in the marriage. They recognize their need for friends. By friends, we don't mean acquaintances, for everyone has many of them. We mean close confidants, those with whom you can be real, unaffected and natural. Without friends, a marriage can become ingrown. We've seen some couples so concerned about their own desires, needs and wants that they become too inwardly focused. Preoccupied with themselves, they seldom reach out to others and thus have a very poor perspective of themselves.

Do you want your mate's perspective of himself to improve? Then encourage him to have friends. Addison wrote, "He who has a good friend needs no mirror." A friend helps your mate see his good qualities and better understand his weaknesses. He reflects your mate's true value and worth, his significance and importance. Like a triple mirror in a dress shop, you and your mate's friends *together* give many positive reflections, which build your mate's self-esteem.

Good friendships reinforce the worth-building that takes place in your marriage. A friend lets your mate know someone else likes him for his ideas, thoughts, and character qualities. At times, your mate may feel that you are committed to him only because you have to be, or that you are prejudiced in a good sort of way. But a friend, an objective third party, can encourage your mate by echoing the very things you've said. Your mate begins to believe your affirming comments because another person has said them, too.

A friend also will stand by your mate when he fails. Laurence Peter said, "You can always tell a real friend. When you've made a fool of yourself, he doesn't feel you've done a permanent job." A true friend is one of a few who can bring value and perspective when your mate has "blown it." Like you, a good friend will "hang in there" when it seems the whole world has walked out. He will exhibit the unconditional love of God.

Job changes, failures and unexpected circumstances can all shake an otherwise settled self-image from its moorings. Life's ups and downs can spawn questions about one's self-worth and confidence. Self-doubt can spread quickly, almost overnight.

Your mate especially needs a friend who will go with him through the difficult seasons of life, such as menopause, the birth of a child, the empty nest, a lost job, mid-life crisis, or difficulty with a teenager. All of life's changing circumstances are handled better with more than one person alongside. A friend can echo your support, belief and confidence in your mate. He can become an outside point of reference amid the storms of life, advising, building up, and giving direction to your mate in ways that you can't, thus strengthening his self-esteem.

A Word to Husbands

Here's a tip for building your wife's self-esteem that will cause her to beam with excitement. Give your wife a weekend off to get away for a friendship-building retreat. Encourage her to ask another woman she already has been getting to know to go with her. Allow her an "expense account" for the weekend, to use as needed in enjoying the time away. On Sunday evening, your wife will return with a better perspective of herself. She'll be encouraged and built up in ways that you, as a man, could never accomplish.

This is especially needed if your marriage is in its early years, and if you have moved and uprooted many of your wife's established friendships. It is also important if she is occupied with small children or works outside the home, leaving little time for developing friendships.

Too many distant peer associations, with no intimate, soul-sharing "sisters," can be a source of comparison, resulting in negative feelings for your wife. Women tend to compare themselves with other women. They compare their appearance, their children's behavior, their work, their cooking, their home decor, their accomplishments and their talents (sewing, singing, teaching, etc.). Your wife needs a friend with whom she can get beyond all these avenues of comparison and competition. She needs a friend with whom she can share her struggles and who won't think less of her or reject her for her feelings.

In my relationship with Dennis, I (Barbara) am confident of his understanding of me, my role and my struggles. We have spent endless hours talking together to create this rapport. He's been with me through many difficult times. He's even played mother with the children when I've been out of the house, so he knows what it is like. But, there is a point beyond which he cannot go. Only another wife and mother can really share the pain I felt in childbirth, as well as my struggles with submission, and can join with me in prayer. Other mothers can provide the support and motivation for the daily weight of raising children that fathers are unable to give.

I need that affinity with two or three women, and I have it. It's wonderful. I am affirmed every time we talk by phone, get together or correspond. And when I feel good about myself, Dennis benefits too. He feels less pressure to meet all my needs.

A wife needs at least one other woman with whom she can identify. This woman is not to take the husband's place as the primary source of approval, but should supplement the self-image you are helping your wife build. Your wife's friend will take your place only if you are not doing your job of loving your wife as Christ intended. So don't be threatened by an outside friendship. Give your wife the time and the encouragement to develop these friendships. You'll not regret it.

A Word to Wives

Wives, allow your husband the time and freedom to develop a close friendship with another man. Most men don't have in-depth relationships with other men. Does your husband? Do you know why he doesn't? Do you understand your man? He struggles with his time, his macho image, and most likely, his inability to know how to relate to another man.

Most men carry images of manhood they've picked up from the media, books and movies, and from their past as they have observed men in their families. Generally, the "strong" men they've seen were not portrayed as being vulnerable. As a result, most men don't have friendships beyond a surface level. What's worse is they don't know how to deepen them.

Because women tend to be naturally more transparent, they form friendships more easily. Men are more inclined to find the added significance a friend provides in pursuits such as business, politics or sports. They speak of having many "friends," while women use that word "friend" more selectively.

Your husband is more vulnerable to self-doubt if his only close friend is you. That doesn't mean your role is not crucial; it means he needs the accountability another man provides, just as you need another woman with whom to relate. So encourage him to share his job and relationship struggles and his questions about life's issues with another man whom he respects. If he is struggling over a particular decision or issue, suggest he get together for breakfast with a Christian man he respects to discuss the problem. You can remind him that he, like you, needs to be real and authentic with a friend. Encourage him to work on letting others inside his life.

"Iron sharpens iron," wrote Solomon, "so one man sharpens another."[1] A good friend will sharpen your husband. He will influence his spiritual growth and counsel him along the way. He will hold him accountable for what he says he'll do. He will be loyal when others are not.

Every Couple Needs a "Couple Friend"

As a couple, you need some "couple friends." You need a relationship in which both the husbands and wives have a special affinity for each other. We prayed for such friends and, for years, tried to find the right "mix." We are thankful that now we feel that affinity for four or five special couples. Some we see frequently, others only occasionally, but the friendships remain solid.

Last summer we spent a portion of our vacation with one such couple. Our friendship has evolved over the past five years because we teach a graduate-level course with them every summer.

We honestly didn't begin this relationship with the goal of becoming intimate friends, but over the years, we've seen God knit our hearts together in a special way. We cherish fond memories of the four of us hiking around a lake, riding horseback through aspen groves and knee-deep flowers and spending casual times sharing dreams, ideas, questions, and concerns. With those pleasant memories comes an occasional phone call or gift — reminders of our value in their lives and theirs in ours. It's hard not to feel good about ourselves when a few choice people know us well and still like us.

Several years ago, we had dinner one evening with a pastor and his wife who are contributing significantly to the Christian community. As we talked, the subject of friends came up. They shared that they maintained an intimate fellowship with three to five couples. These people were committed to a lifetime friendship. They didn't all live in the same town or go to the same church, but they knew they could count on these friends to be there when the going got tough. It was a mutual understanding.

Do you have couple friends? Individual friends? Ask God to direct you in developing both types of essential relationships. Spend time with the people to whom He leads you. Get to know them and share yourselves. Be honest and open. Communicate your love for them and your commitment to them as your friends. The blessing will be mutual.

In the past fifteen years, I (Dennis) have experienced two very dark days in my life, two periods of time when I really questioned my worth as a man. Both were problems in my work that caused me to question my effectiveness as a leader. They were times of self-doubt, discouragement and emotional turmoil.

Fortunately, I had two very godly friends with whom I had been developing relationships. I had helped them at their points of crisis, and now I needed them. It was difficult to admit my need to them, but thanks to Barbara's encouragement, I opened myself up and asked for their advice, counsel and help.

These two men stood by me and, along with Barbara, reminded me of the truth about myself. It was difficult to believe at first, but slowly, over a period of time, their lives and words made a difference in my life. Their acceptance, counsel and wisdom were invaluable. Their gifts of their time communicated to me that I had value. Their belief in me as a man told me I was O.K. even in this particular situation.

That's friendship. It's a joy, a risk, a responsibility. It's also a comfort to know people want to be with you, whether you are rich or poor, sloppy or immaculate, famous or unknown. Friends support your self-esteem.

So do yourself and your mate a giant favor. Broaden your friendships and, thus, your horizons. Develop some lasting friendships and watch how these allies assist you in building your mate's self-esteem. They will preserve the work you've done and accelerate the growth of your mate's self-image.

ESTEEM BUILDER PROJECT

(Use a sheet of paper if necessary.)

1. Inventory all your mate's friendships. Who is his best friend of the same sex (one or two)?
2. Give your mate and his friend a weekend retreat to talk, shop, hunt, etc.
3. As a couple, over the next six to twelve months, pray and ask God to direct you to one or two couples with whom you would like to pursue a friendship. Then begin to cultivate that relationship by spending time with them.

Keeping Life Manageable

Completing the construction of your mate's self-image requires making tough decisions, knowing your values, thinking prayerfully, and keeping life simple.

— 13 —
Getting the Ice Off
Your Balloon

- Burned-Out, Strung-Out, and Wrung-Out
- Life Can Get Weighty
- Going Up or Going Down
- Which Way Is Your Mate's Balloon Headed?
- Self-Image and Simple Living
- Winning Where It Counts the Most
- Helpful Hints to Keep Life Manageable
  - Getting Rid of Excess Baggage
  - Know Your Values
  - Think Prayerfully
  - Keep Life Balanced
- Esteem Builder Project

Building Block 9: Keeping Life Manageable

WOODY ALLEN HAS SAID, "Eighty percent of success is showing up." He may be right. But today too many people are "showing up" absolutely exhausted by the logistics of their frenzied lifestyles. They are unable to do anything more than show up.

In conversations with friends, have you noticed recurring statements (said with a sigh) such as, "We are just so busy these days," or, "As soon as this month is over, our schedule will lighten up, and then we'll get together"? As a culture, we are forever in a hurry — rushing, pushing, frantically cramming more into an already swollen schedule.

It seems as though most people want to get off this merry-go-round, but few are willing to throw the switch and make some hard decisions. As a result, many people are burned-out, strung-out and wrung-out by their drive for significance. Instead of getting anywhere, they simply get exhausted. They discover, as Samuel Butler said, "Life is one long process of getting tired."

What about your mate? Does his lifestyle contribute to his self-esteem or merely to his fatigue? Perhaps, as you build him up, you will need to aid him in eliminating some nonessentials from his schedule.

Life Can Get Weighty

A good friend confided in us recently, "Life used to be so simple. Now, well, it seems so complex. There are the children, work demands and pressures, bills, home maintenance, friendships, church responsibilities, social obligations, long-term financial planning, and . . . well, the list seems to go on forever. I can't win for losing. I feel like I'm drowning, and my mate doesn't seem to be helping. Instead of helping me float, she is sinking, too. In fact, my mate keeps pulling me down."

Maybe you've felt like our friend — emotionally sinking under the weight of it all. His sinking feeling reminds us of a story that I (Dennis) wrote in "My Soapbox" (our monthly newsletter to Family Life Conference alumni), a story that illustrates what is taking place in many marriages.

Going Up or Going Down?

"Three thousand forbidding miles stood between three men in a balloon called Double Eagle II and Europe. Presque Isle, Maine, was covered with darkness as a handful of hopefuls huddled around the helium-filled balloon. Silently, the Double Eagle II inched its way upward. Men and nature would battle again in man's attempt to cross the Atlantic in a balloon. The men waved good-bye as they started their journey through what was to be a precarious invisible corridor to Europe. Two previous attempts had failed; miraculously, all had survived.

"Soaring by day and drifting downward at night, the crew masterfully rode those winds like an imaginary angel for three nights and two days. Then, a few hundred miles off the coast of Ireland, the weather changed as ominous, gray clouds surrounded them. Ice crystals, twinkling with deceptive beauty, began to form on the balloon, which rose five stories above them. Soon sheets of ice weighing thousands of pounds forced the giant balloon downward.

"Panic replaced peacefulness as the crew watched the altimeter tell the story . . . 24,000 feet . . . 20,000 . . . 16,000 . . . 12,000. With no solar rays to melt the ice, the crew believed they were headed for an unwelcome baptism. All excess weight had to be eliminated. Frantically, the ballast was dumped. Books, canned foods, and other equipment were shoved over into the Atlantic. The ice pushed them down further . . . to 8,000 . . . 6,000. They radioed, "Mayday! Mayday! Mayday!" along with their position. They tossed overboard a video camera they'd hoped to use to record their landing. Finally, they reluctantly jettisoned their marine radio as they fought to remain airborne.

"Three frightened men watched helplessly as the rolling angry Atlantic came up to meet them . . . 4,000 . . . then suddenly — Eureka! They leveled out and broke through the grey mist into sunshine. The balloon soared as the warm rays melted the sheets of ice.

"Crossing the jagged coast of Ireland, they floated above rolling green hills and then the English Channel. Thousands of cars lined the farm roads of France as the Double Eagle II came to rest in a cornfield a few miles from Paris and the airport where Lindberg had landed a half-century before them. They had made it!"[1]

Which Way Is Your Mate's Balloon Headed?

Is your mate's balloon soaring smoothly? Can you spot which way it is headed before it gets too close to the sea? Is there ice on it? What is causing the ice to form? Is your mate's balloon going down too rapidly? Will you help him remove those burdens, or will you add more weight? Most likely, you are strategic to your mate's "weight" problem.

Self-Image and Simple Living

Remember, your mate's self-image is how he thinks and feels about himself in light of his internal expectations (the phantom). If your mate is personally insecure, he may be attempting to fill that vacuum of insecurity in his self-image by crowding his life with activity. Busyness boosts his self-importance by making him feel needed by many. Discontentment

HELPFUL HINTS

Here are some suggestions that we have found beneficial in keeping life manageable for the Rainey household:

- You can't always please everyone, but you should please those you value the most. Determine whom you wish to please and live accordingly.
- Pressure and stress can be a result of responsibility. By discarding a responsibility or two, you can lighten your load and reduce some pressure. Since God has placed us here to "rule,"[2] ridding ourselves of all responsibility is not an alternative. Doing what He's called you to do, however, and depending on Him in the process will put pressure in perspective.
- Avoid comparison at all costs. It only breeds discontent, envy, and drivenness.
- Practice saying, "No, I'm sorry, I can't do that," at least once a day. The word *no* can be a powerful crowbar in dislodging other people's control over your life and schedule. (By the way, you don't owe people an excuse!)
- Learn to settle for limited, achievable objectives. We have learned we usually expect too much from ourselves in any given 24-hour day. REMEMBER: YOU HAVE ALL THE TIME YOU NEED TO DO EVERYTHING GOD WANTS YOU TO DO!

and comparison drive him to add more activities to his already overcrowded schedule.

Blurred by a life that is often out of control, he loses his focus and sense of priorities. Ultimately, he experiences failure, further damaging his self-image.

Winning Where It Counts

Unfortunately, we are not exempt from this temptation to overextend ourselves. We struggle with schedules, goals and expectations about life and priorities. Like yours, our days are full from the first ring of the alarm to the last light out at night. With our children all in different stages of development, it gets pretty crazy at times. Our schedule can get away from us, but we work together to avoid living under the peril of the urgent. We have determined to win where it counts the most: at home.

We try, but we don't always succeed. We make plenty of mistakes, but we are fighting the current, not ignoring it or going along with it. One of our mutual commitments is to assist each other in this area. In the process, we're learning, growing and getting wiser. We have to if we're going to win at home.

Nobody Does It All

Because we have six children, we repeatedly are asked, "How do you do it all?"

Our answer is simple. "We do *not* do it *all*." That six-word sentence has been a boxcar full of help for us. Admitting the obvious is liberating. It may help you and your mate, too.

Guess what? No one else "does it all" either. Because a person does one or two things well does not automatically mean he does everything well. No one can, so why should *you* try? Your phantom may give you the idea that you have to have your life perfectly together, but don't believe it. Relax and repeat with us, "We do not do it all."

As individuals and as a couple we have areas where we continue to fall short. At times we feel like "social nerds." We don't go out with friends or invite people into our home as much as we'd like. The flower beds are filled with an odd assortment of weeds; rooms are unpainted; chairs are in need of repair . . . and just take a look at Dennis's garage or Barbara's sewing room. This "season" in our marriage will pass, however, and someday these two social nerds will come out of the closet and make their debut.

But other objectives must be accomplished first. As a friend's needlepoint wall hanging reads, "A clean house is a sign of a life misspent." It's not that a clean house is wrong, but in God's economy, it may not be as important as other values. We have chosen to follow the priority of God's call and His values. God has given us a ministry and a large family, and they determine the majority of our time commitments. Therefore, our daily lives are governed, not by phantom expectations or comparison with others, but by God's plan.

The Bible teaches we are to live in obedience to God's plan for our lives. The Scriptures also teach that life is to be lived joyfully — not with our jaw set and our teeth clenched, hanging on as if we were in a wind tunnel. Joy is part of God's plan for us.

Life can be compared to a marathon run — long distance and cross country. It demands that we be wise in the way we run. We must follow the pace determined by our coach, the God of heaven. Among the ancient Greeks, the runner who won the marathon was not the first man to cross the finish line, but the first man to cross it with his torch still burning. If your mate tries to run the race of life at too frantic a pace, he may be in danger of extinguishing the torch of his spiritual life — his relationship with God — and thus damaging his self-image.

So what's the solution?

Getting Rid of Excess Baggage

Just as the crew of the Double Eagle II had to dump much of its excess baggage to survive, you may have to lighten your load. You and your mate may have so many activities and responsibilities going simultaneously that your marriage, like the helium balloon, may be falling. We recommend that you join us in periodically checking your marriage altimeter.

Early in our marriage, we were driving together to Cincinnati on a business trip. Barbara was distressed because she was not accomplishing all that she did when she was single. I asked her to go over her "to do" list with me as we made the two-hour journey.

I'll never forget that list. It was overwhelming. I felt distressed for her. She had more to do than three people could have accomplished. Cooking, sewing, quilting, cleaning, watercolor painting, laundry, reading, grocery shopping, writing letters, entertaining, Bible study, doing things with me — all adding to an already overcrowded schedule. And she was pregnant. She was totally drained by the first trimester of pregnancy. None of her objectives were being reached, and she was feeling like a failure. Together we prioritized her list and began to eliminate some nonessentials. Barbara was just as busy as ever, but she was relieved to know she didn't have to do "everything."

That was the first of many similar discussions that followed in our marriage relationship. We both tend to expect too much of ourselves and as a result we sometimes consider ourselves to have failed. Usually the impression of failing is from within and simply is not true. It results from holding to a standard that couldn't be achieved by Superman or Superwoman.

We've found that a proper perspective on scheduling and expectations about what can be accomplished is tough to maintain. Life can get out of control, and, like a runaway train, it can be very destructive in the end. So periodically we get away and check our expectations about life. It is very beneficial to sit together and analyze all that we expect of ourselves and of each other, as well as what others expect of us.

Likewise, you can help your mate scale down expectations to reasonable standards. Take time out to help align your mate's schedule, overhaul his goals, and establish his priorities *before* the ride gets rough.

This past summer, a pair of flying enthusiasts revealed their plans to build a homemade plane that would be the first to fly nonstop around the world. To utilize every cubic inch of space, their only "companions" on the twenty-day flight would be food, water and fuel — nothing extra could be allowed.

In a similar way, we need to be wise about what we take with us on our journey through life. Paul writes, "Therefore be careful how you walk, not as unwise men, but as wise, making the most of your time, because the days are evil. So then do not be foolish, but understand what the will of the Lord is."[3]

Wisdom. It evaluates life by God's standards. It looks at life through God's eyes. Wisdom looks frequently at the circumstances of life and then consults God and His Word for the right response.

Evaluate your life and marriage with prudence. What does the altimeter say? Is your mate's altimeter climbing or falling? Is there a break coming in your mate's schedule, or is his pace nonstop? Check your own altitude, too. Wisdom may tell you that it's time to throw some excess baggage overboard in both your lives.

Know Your Values

A prerequisite for helping your mate know what to throw overboard is knowing his value system (and yours). Together, evaluate those standards in relation to God's values (see the accompanying Inventory and Analysis). Understanding your mate's standards will explain why he gives his time to certain things. Articulating your ideals to one another will help you and your mate see what you should reasonably expect out of life. Discuss and determine how you should schedule your time so that it is achievable and reasonable for both partners.

The first time we listed and compared our top five values, we were quite surprised. One of mine (Dennis's) was developing relationships; one of Barbara's was hard work. Interestingly, neither of us had listed the other's values on our list. It wasn't that I didn't believe in hard work or that Barbara didn't think relationships were important; we just saw other things as more important to each of us at that time in our lives. Since then, we have spent many hours discussing our individual values, those things we hold very dear to our hearts. As we have matured, many of them have changed in importance.

VALUES INVENTORY AND ANALYSIS

Determine your mate's values by following these steps:

1. Pick an evening with at least one hour of guaranteed quiet. (Put your phone-answering machine on and turn off the front porch light.)
2. Spend five to ten minutes individually listing the top five values you hold as most important.
3. Compare lists.
4. Ask your mate "Why?" for each item he listed. Find out his reasons for his choices. Discuss your differences.
5. Date and keep both lists.
6. Watch his schedule, activities, and free time to see if it "matches" his list. Does his expenditure of time match his top five values? How can you help him live according to his values?
7. Schedule another values analysis in a year.

Now when we plan our goals together, which are a reflection of our values, we each understand what is important to the other. As a result, our objectives and priorities have begun to demonstrate principles that both of us have brought to the marriage.

Think Prayerfully

Take time with your mate to get alone and think and to listen to God. Also give your mate time alone to do this. Ideally, you and your mate should get away together for a long weekend at least once a year with no business agenda on the side. Then you can think clearly because you have time. Take a nap. Go for a walk in the woods together. Talk about your life and contemplate the direction it's going. Do you like where you are headed? What do you want it to look like in a few years? What are your goals over the next five years? You can't plan or set goals and priorities without first taking time to think and pray.

Set aside Sunday as a day of rest. Within the Ten Commandments, God has provided a long-standing truth that our modern culture is ignoring, to its detriment. The Sabbath was to be a day set apart unto God — a day of rest to refuel our perspective and refresh our communion with Him. As a result of our decision to try to do this, we have begun to reap the enriching qualities of a clear mind, a relaxed spirit and the knowledge that our life is well-pleasing to God. (Gordon MacDonald, in his book, *Ordering Your Private World,* has an entire chapter on this subject, which we recommend for your reading.)

Keep Life Balanced

Just as high-wire artists must maintain a precarious balance, so Christians must balance their walk. Living a balanced life requires concentration, observation and corrections along the way — some minute, others drastic.

You and your mate may be too reclusive, too cautious, living in a rut. You may need to step out on the wire and take some risks. God did not give us life to bore us, but to provide opportunities to trust Him and to grow in faith.

But, possibly you and your mate continue to live an unreasonable lifestyle, never getting off the merry-go-round to evaluate all that you're doing. Like us, you may need to assess your life regularly to keep it on target.

Keeping life balanced will give your mate the benefit of self-control. Over the long haul, you will see your mate's load lightened and his productivity increased. His self-image will be strengthened immensely if you help him keep a reasonable schedule. You *can* make a difference in your mate's life by keeping life simple and manageable.

ESTEEM BUILDER PROJECT
(Use separate sheets of paper as necessary.)

1. As a couple, list all your activities under one of the two areas shown, then evaluate them.

Those We Can Control	Those We Cannot Control
_____	_____
_____	_____
_____	_____
_____	_____
_____	_____
_____	_____
_____	_____

2. Go back through your lists and highlight those things which tend to be pulling you or your mate down. Discuss your solution. Can you or should you help by taking responsibility? Should his list be scaled down or modified? How does your list affect him?
3. Assist your mate in prioritizing his list. Where must he succeed? Ask him to discuss with you how you can protect him and help him "win."

Discovering Dignity Through Destiny

True significance is found as we invest in a cause
that will outlive us.

— 14 —
Leaving a Legacy
That Will Outlive You

- Vision — What Is It?
- Ask Yourself Some Tough Questions
- You and Your Mate Are His Workmanship
- A Man With a Destiny
- Finding Your Destiny Is a Process
- Helping Your Mate Gain a Sense of Destiny
- Look Behind Him
- Inventory Your Mate's Talents
- Instigate Truth-Speaking
- Believe It, Risk It, Live It
- Leaving a Legacy
- Dignity Through Destiny
- Esteem Builder Project

Building Block 10: Discovering Dignity Through Destiny

HELEN KELLER WAS once asked, "Is there anything worse than being blind?" She replied, "Yes. The most pathetic person in the whole world is someone who has sight but has no vision."

Vision. What is it? It is possessing a sense of purpose in life. It's seeing ahead into the uncharted future and knowing where you're going. Vision is leaving a mark on the present by visualizing the future. Jonathan Swift said in 1699, "Vision is the art of seeing the invisible."

Vision doesn't come easily. Your mate needs you to help bring a sense of vision, direction and purpose to his life. In helping him in that way, you will also help him improve his self-image. For when your mate's purpose is elevated above

189

the temporal, his personal dignity and esteem receive a promotion.

Feelings of significance, one of the pillars of a positive self-esteem, are seldom found in a wandering person, a nomad with few roots, drifting through life. But a person with a sense of personal destiny has confidence and pride in himself. He knows he has been chosen, hand-picked, set apart from the rest of humanity for a dignified purpose.

Just as the President of the United States is selected from a field of many for the paramount task of leadership, so you and your mate have been chosen by God to fulfill His customized plan in your marriage, family and world. Have you caught that vision? Has your mate?

In this chapter, we will address you and your mate as individuals and as a couple. Though God may at times call you to separate causes, you have a destiny and purpose as a couple. As you together commit yourselves to God's holy and high purpose, you will realize the significance of your marriage.

Ask Yourself Some Tough Questions

The American culture of the late twentieth century has been defined as narcissistic, selfish, dependent and crowd-following. We are a people living for the moment, unmindful of the future.

Many individuals, and most couples, are not asking enough questions about life. Caught up in the rush of living life, they seldom take enough time to get out of the mainstream to look at where they are headed. Seneca said, "You must know for which harbor you are headed if you are to catch the right wind to take you there." Do you and your mate know where you are going?

Ask yourself:
- What is my vision, direction, purpose and pursuit in life?
- What is my mate's vision, direction and purpose?
- What is God's ordained destiny for my mate? For me? For my marriage? For my family?

Can you answer these questions? Are you confident in your answers? Perhaps you and your mate are searching for your purpose, direction and vision in life. Or maybe neither of you has given much thought to your destiny. Perhaps you are not going anywhere, but are drifting directionless, visionless, and purposeless.

Will Rogers warned, "Even if you're on the right track, you'll get run over if you just sit there!" You and your mate may be Christians and "on the right track," but you also have to be moving toward something — deciding on a daily basis how to use the life God has granted. Why not gain God's vision for your life? Why not determine His "call," individually and as a couple?

Your vision, or call, probably will include accomplishments and relationships. Whatever that vision, dream or goal encompasses, it will give context and meaning to minor decisions as well as to major forks in the road.

Determining your direction is like developing a sixth sense: the sense of faith. Through it you begin first to grasp the unseen, and then to put it into practice. You and your mate will develop self-confidence as you fulfill God's unique plan for your lives. You both will begin to see and feel your importance in God's eyes as you discover your importance in His plan. You will feel valued and needed by the one whose opinion counts most.

You and Your Mate Are His Workmanship

Paul spoke of this direction and vision in Ephesians 2:10: "For we are His workmanship, created in Christ Jesus for good works, which God prepared beforehand, that we should walk in them."

Is Paul speaking of a definite plan by God for an individual's life? We believe so. Look again at the verse:

"For we are His workmanship,	*God made us*
created in Christ Jesus	*He redeemed us*
for good works,	*our purpose*
which God prepared beforehand,	*God's plan*
that we should walk in them."	*our responsibility*

This is all part of the divine master plan for humanity. God is accomplishing His perfect work and His perfect plan through imperfect people. And He wants to use you and your mate to accomplish His plan. In return, your life will reflect great value, worth, significance and dignity as you yield to God and participate with Him in His "good works."

Can you think of anything more satisfying than fulfilling the creator's design for your life? To fulfill the purpose for which you and your mate were created and brought together will bring the ultimate dignity to your lives.

A Man With a Destiny

A man who lived in England in the second half of the eighteenth century illustrates the principle of destiny. At the age of twenty-one, William Wilberforce was elected to Parliament. He was a small man, barely over five feet tall, but his natural ability as an orator made him a giant.

In the fall of 1785, Wilberforce made a decision that changed his life. An old friend diligently instructed him and debated with him regarding the Scriptures and Jesus Christ, and John Newton (author of "Amazing Grace") gave him counsel. The choice was clear.

Two years following his decision to follow Jesus Christ, Wilberforce wrote in his diary, "Almighty God has set before me two great objectives: the abolition of the slave trade, and the reformation of manners."[1]

As a young Christian, he had seen the injustice of a trade that depended on the sale of human beings. He wondered if God had saved him only to take him to heaven, or did He have more in mind? Did God have a plan for his life, a place for him to serve? His conscience was pricked. The evil of slavery must be met head-on in Parliament. Heeding John Newton's advice to remain in public office, he set out to remove the blight from his homeland using his political position.

Wilberforce knew it would be a bitter battle against the wealthy businessmen whose fortunes were built on slave trading. It's doubtful, however, that he could have foreseen the long years of repeated defeat and discouragement ahead of him. He and his compatriots were ridiculed and derided, but they remained faithful to the cause that burned in their hearts.

After twenty years of repeatedly introducing a bill to abolish slavery, Wilberforce saw the House of Commons and the House of Lords pass the bill in 1807. But the effects of his efforts reached even further. A great spiritual movement spread across England. Many members of Parliament had become committed Christians during those twenty years, and other reforms to aid the oppressed began to grow.

In 1797, Wilberforce wrote about his views of Christianity, "I must confess equally boldly that my own solid hopes for the well-being of my country depend, not so much on her navies and armies, nor on the wisdom of her rulers, nor on the spirit of her people, as on the persuasion that she still contains many who love and obey the Gospel of Christ."[2]

William Wilberforce had a mandate from God and a vision for his country. He was not content just to wear the title of Christian; he felt he must *live* it.

In your life as a couple, as in Wilberforce's life, long-range goals can keep the fires of perseverance burning during the downpours of short-term disappointments. A dream — a vision — can help keep hope alive, even after repeated failures.

Finding Your Destiny Is a Process

Finding a personal destiny as a couple is progressive. Time is essential to its discovery, as is obedience to God's call. What does God want you to do as a couple? Is your Christianity to be merely a personal matter, or should it reach out to others? How? God may not lead you to champion a cause, as He did Wilberforce, but He may want you to join with others who already are leading offensives. Wilberforce did not act alone. Many joined him. He needed those fellow believers to stand with him. Likewise, God may have someone or some cause for you and your mate, and perhaps your whole family, to stand behind.

Whether you and your mate fill an "up front" position or work "behind the scenes," you will find dignity in doing God's work. Position has nothing to do with significance.

We have found that nothing holds greater significance for us than being the couple God has called us to be and accomplishing the work He has laid before us.

Helping Your Mate Gain a Sense of Destiny

Horoscopes do not determine your mate's destiny. No soothsayer or palm reader can prophesy your future. But *you* can guide your mate in discovering God's direction for his life. Not only do you share that call with him, but God also has uniquely positioned you to work with your mate to accomplish it. By being an encouraging coach to your mate, you not only aid in discerning God's direction, but also help sustain that direction over a lifetime.

Before you embark on this quest, you must understand and carry with you a couple of perspectives. Without them, you would be like a miner going into a gold or silver mine to search for precious metals with no hard hat, pick or flashlight.

First, God is intricately and ingeniously involved in creation. He knows the grains of sand in the ocean,[3] the names of all the stars,[4] the number of hairs on your head and the very instant every little sparrow dies.[5] If He knows the tiny details from the bottom of the ocean to the ends of the universe, then we can correctly assume He knows what is going on in between.

Second, God is sovereign. He is fully in charge. You will find no personal destiny, either for your mate or for you both as a couple, apart from an inner confidence that there is a God who sovereignly rules. And since He rules, all of life has purpose. Consequently, He has a divine design for each individual life. You both are significant in God's design.

What is the purpose of His reign? What goals is He accomplishing? Clearly, God's overall plan is to redeem humanity to Himself. Incredibly, He has chosen to use men and women like you and like us to execute His plan of affecting eternity.

As you talk together of the greatness of God and the unspeakable privilege of being chosen by Him, your mate's self-esteem will quietly grow in strength. And just as the reward of gold and silver awaits those who persevere in mining, so a lasting reward is being built and stored in heaven for those who find and obey God's call and plan for their lives. The promise of a heavenly reward is motivation enough to live our lives on earth in obedience to Him.

Take the challenge of eternal reward to heart. Arm yourself with the right perspective of God and His sovereignty, and begin to search for your mate's destiny and your own.

DISCOVERING YOUR MATE'S DESTINY

1. Look behind him.

Begin helping your mate find his destiny by first looking in the past. Watch for qualities that God has built into your mate's life to prepare him uniquely for a particular task. What cause or idea continues to surface in your mate's thinking and conversation? What injustice makes him angry? What burdens his heart about your town, your state, your world? What desires have been a part of your mate's life for years and, when channeled into God's overall plan for man, would bring great ministry to others? Don't expect immediate answers to these questions. Remember, it's a process; it requires time.

We did not arrive at our present field of ministry overnight. Initially, we worked with high school students, helping win them to Christ and beginning the process of discipleship in their lives through Bible studies.

During those years, we made some interesting observations. Many times a student would express an interest in spiritual things, only to go home and face discouragement from his parents. At other times a student's spiritual growth would be negatively affected by a divorced mother or father. We began to see the need to help marriages so the children would not suffer. We also saw the need to do everything we could to strengthen our own marriage. As a result, five years after we married, we began to work in the area of marriage and the family.

Is your mate burdened by education, government, business, the hungry, the poor, the family, the church, prayer, giving, the needs of Third World countries, or ministering to the sick? Why not ask your mate what he would do if he knew he could not fail?

In 1776, during the Revolutionary War, a young man was captured for spying on the British. His response to his captors has never been forgotten in our land. Nathan Hale said, "I only regret that I have but one life to give for my country." If your mate had a choice, for what cause would he be willing to give his life?

Often, God will use a life given to Him to affect future generations beyond what can be seen at present. One example is the role of motherhood. Today it has been relegated to a low level of importance, but in God's design, it has great destiny. Other humbling servant tasks are looked down upon as well, but if God has called your mate to fill one of them, then it is an honor. No destiny is insignificant if it comes from our sovereign God. And your mate will earn reward in heaven if he fulfills his destiny — whatever it is — with a spirit of joy and contentment in obedience to Christ.

2. Inventory his talents.

In Matthew 25 Jesus told the parable of the talents to his disciples. A master gave to each of his three servants a certain number of talents. The master rewarded the servants who faithfully used and invested the talents they were given, but the one who buried his talent and did not use it, had it taken away.

By observing, you can notice and then help your mate discover his talents, abilities and spiritual gifts (those unique areas of spiritual capability, listed in Romans 12 and 1 Corinthians 12). With increased confidence, he can be a more faithful servant and use the talents that God has given him to further His kingdom.

Encourage your mate to faithfulness in what you both already know he does well. Beware of adding expectations that are too many or too high. Your mate doesn't have to do everything all at once. He can spend a lifetime investing those talents for the good of man and for heavenly reward.

As you assess your mate's talents, both of you probably will feel the need for outside help. Ask friends who know your mate well to give their opinions. Ask your pastor or another mature Christian whom you know well for ideas.

Proverbs 2:1-5 talks about seeking, searching and finding wisdom. You will need it if you are to answer these questions. Wisdom, as we have stated previously, is skill in everyday living according to God's patterns and blueprints. As you go through the process with your mate, ask God to grant wisdom to handle the many forks in the road which you will encounter.

We can't promise quick answers or simple solutions. (Our own lives didn't begin to have focus until we turned thirty.) But we can promise that your interest and encouragement can have a great deal to do with assisting your mate as he distills his destiny.

3. Instigate truth-speaking.

Your mate's destiny is in the future, but it is shaped and fulfilled by daily choices. This is illustrated in the biblical account of Israel's history.

God constantly told the nation of Israel that they were a special people. The Jews knew they were set apart for a unique, significant contribution to mankind. That helped build national unity, and they were excited about who they were and where they were headed. But what they chose to believe individually about themselves and their relationship with God made a big difference in their personal participation in God's plan.

One thing we most remember about the Israelites is that they "grumbled in their tents."[6] They fussed and complained, and generally felt sorry for themselves. Through their negative self-talk, they convinced themselves that God had forgotten them, and they lost their sense of destiny as a nation.

Negative self-talk can do the same to us today. If we tell ourselves that God has forgotten us, or that He doesn't know what He's doing, we, too, are "grumbling in our tents." Our internal conversations can express discontent and dissatisfaction with the present. Even though God has chosen us, we can convince ourselves that our destiny is no different from the average person's.

Negative self-talk says things such as, "I don't have any talents God could use"; "My life won't amount to much"; or "I'm just one person in five million." Some of the people of Israel were convinced through negative self-talk that God had deserted them in the wilderness. They liberally spread their germs of grumbling around until the whole nation was infected.

In the same way, your mate's negative self-talk can be very convincing. Your mate may believe, on the basis of his feelings, that God can't be God in a particular situation. If you join him in agreement, you will lose your sense of destiny as a couple, as well as your hope for living.

But self-talk can be positive, too. For example, when our children are afraid, we ask them to tell us what the truth is: that Daddy and Mommy love them and will protect them, and Jesus loves them and will protect them. Then we remind them of a song, or a verse in the Bible, or we pray with them.

I (Barbara) used similar self-talk several years ago when I went through a time of being fearful whenever Dennis was out of town. I went to sleep at night by repeating a couple of verses from Proverbs that reminded me of the truth: God is in control, and He cares for me. That's positive self-talk, and it has positive results.

Proverbs 23:7 says, "For as he [a man or a woman] thinks within himself, so he is." Encourage your mate not only not to say negative things out loud, but also not even to *think* them. Your mate may have a habit of saying negative things about himself out of his lack of positive self-esteem. He may be "begging" for your support and affirmation. Respond to those pessimistic words with sympathy, understanding, and a good dose of the truth. Help your mate see how negative self-talk affects him and his relationship with God.

4. Adopt a "corporate" family pride.

A recent business magazine article listed the most admired corporations in America. Those listed had developed an identity that consumers recognized as one of excellence and of trustworthiness. IBM was number one . . . again.

If you have a friend who works for IBM, you know its employees have great corporate pride in what they do. This pride is contagious, spreading feelings of worth throughout the organization.

In a similar way, your marriage ought to embrace a sense of "corporate family pride." Not a haughty, rebellious-toward-God pride, but a sense of true respect and admiration for what God has done for you and your family.

Our family pride is not vanity or conceit, but a statement that this marriage and family are an integral part of what God is accomplishing for mankind. We don't feel that we are better than other families, only that there is no better place for any of us to be. We have great family dignity because we are doing what God has called us to do. No other marriage or family has a call identical to ours. We are truly unique — very special.

And so are you.

Reflecting back over the more than fourteen years that we have sought to be used by God enhances our family's identity even further. Sometimes the fog of feeling insignificant will lift, almost instantly, as we recall all God has done in our lives and what He has used us to accomplish.

If you aren't already doing so, we challenge you to begin thinking in new terms about your life, your partner, your marriage and your family. A positive family identity will spread infectiously to all its members.

5. Believe it; risk it; live it.

As your "divine destiny" begins to emerge, it will demand action. Action demands risk. And risk demands faith — your faith and your mate's faith. Resolve together to fulfill your God-given call to the best of your ability. Find your place to serve.

- Is it through some community service project?
- Is it in the local church?
- Is your present place at home with the children?
- Is there a ministry you can volunteer to help?
- Do you need to make a vocational/career change?

God usually doesn't reveal His whole plan at once. When we make a commitment, He gives us light, a little at a time, to encourage us to walk by faith. Then, when we have walked that far, He gives us more light.

Leaving a Legacy

A husband and wife who walked by faith and, consequently, left a legacy far beyond what they even imagined, lived in the early 1700s in colonial America. Their names were Jonathan and Sarah Edwards.

Jonathan Edwards felt God's call to become a minister. He and his young bride began a pastorate in a small congregation. In the years that followed, he wrote many sermons, prayers and books, and was influential in beginning the Great Awakening. Together they produced eleven children who grew to adulthood. Sarah was a partner in her husband's ministry, and he sought her advice regarding sermons and church matters. They spent time talking about these things together, and, when their children were old enough, they included them in the discussions.

The effects of their lives have been far-reaching, but the most measurable results of their faithfulness to God's call is found through their descendants. Elizabeth Dodds records a study done by A. E. Winship in 1900 in which he lists a few of the accomplishments of the 1,400 Edwards descendants he was able to find:[7]

- 100 lawyers and a dean of a law school
- 80 holders of public office
- 66 physicians and a dean of a medical school
- 65 professors of colleges and universities
- 30 judges
- 13 college presidents
- 3 mayors of large cities

- 3 governors of states
- 3 United States senators
- 1 controller of the United States Treasury
- 1 vice president of the United States

What kind of legacy will you and your mate leave? Will it be lasting, as was the Edwards'? Will it be imperishable and eternal? Or will you leave behind only perishable things: buildings, money, possessions?

The apostle Paul instructed Timothy to invest his life in *faithful* men who would be able to pass the truth on to the next generation.[8] Where does God want you and your mate to invest the time you have been given?

Dignity Through Destiny

David Livingstone, the missionary to Africa, said, "I will go anywhere, as long as it is forward." And by moving forward and advancing God's kingdom, he undoubtedly also advanced his sense of dignity.

Gaining a vision and a direction in life will yield significance in your life as well, especially if that heading and direction has been set by the omnipotent God of the universe. In fact, true vision, direction and destiny can come only from the one who controls not only the present but also the future.

By discovering your eternal destiny, you will begin to build a lasting dignity in your lives. The internal awareness of that dignity will enhance the self-esteem of every member of your family.

The challenge is the same for all of us. Will we follow Christ and fulfill His call and vision for our lives? Just as we found life in no other person than Jesus Christ, so we find a dignity like no other in the destiny that He provides.

ESTEEM BUILDER PROJECT
(Use a sheet of paper if necessary.)

1. Begin to discover your destiny as a couple by talking and dreaming together about what you wish you could do with your lives. What areas, issues, and needs of people would you like to affect? Take notes of your conversations. Pray that in the weeks and months to come God will guide your conversations and begin to reveal His leading to you.

2. If you already have a sense of vision and destiny, write out your vision for *your* life (be specific). Ask your mate to do the same for *himself.*

3. Review each other's statements and respond to what you each have written.

4. Together, begin to determine your family's vision and how you can establish a "corporate family pride."

Five Investment Tips

Investing in your wife will prove profitable and will bring lasting assets.

1. Treat Her as a Participating Partner
2. Protect Her
3. Honor Her
4. Develop Her Gifts and Horizons as a Woman
5. Assist in Problem Solving

— 15 —

Five Investment Tips
That Will Yield a Great Return

- "No Worse Than Anyone Else"
- The Wise Investment
- Treat Your Wife as a Full Participating Partner
- Protect Your Wife
- Techniques to Honor Your Wife
- Hats a Wife Wears
- Develop Her Gifts and Horizons as a Woman
- Assist in Problem Solving
- Persevere With Your Investment
- Barbara's Tips to Men
- Esteem Builder Project

Man to Man: From Dennis

TOM PETERS, AUTHOR of the best-selling book, *In Search of Excellence,* was once exhorting a group of corporate officers toward excellence. He spoke to these leaders for several hours, challenging them to raise their standards. Finally, a top executive, irritated by much of what Peters had said, interrupted him to voice his dissatisfaction.

"Peters, I'm tired of hearing all this stuff on excellence!" he began. "We don't need this! Our company is *no worse than anyone else's.*"

Outwardly, Peters passively listened to this corporate leader continue his tirade. But inwardly, his mind was racing: *Now wouldn't that statement make a great byline right under the*

company's logo — 'International Widgets . . . We're no worse than anyone else'![1]
As men, our attitude can be very similar to that corporate leader's. Exasperated with all the areas in which we have to give leadership, we might exclaim, "I'm tired of hearing what I need to be doing, where I'm failing as a husband, and everything that's wrong in our marriage. After all, *our* marriage is no worse than anyone else's!"

Although you may have felt that way on occasion, as I have, I'm confident you wouldn't want to proudly display a sign in your front yard declaring that motto. And, as the leader of your wife, you recognize that you (along with the rest of us) can use some advice or counsel in knowing exactly what to do next. You need a few solid "investment tips" if you are to see the "stock" of your wife's self-image soar in value.

When I was twenty and a sophomore in college, I got a hot investment tip from a stockbroker. I'll never forget Dashew Business Machines (no relation to International Business Machines, I can assure you). Without getting my dad's advice, I invested $500 in four hundred shares. After all, it was coming out of bankruptcy, so it had no place to go but up. It couldn't go lower than $1.25 per share . . . or so I thought.

My baptism into Wall Street was a harsh one. Dashew went from $1.25 to $.87, to $.50, to $.12, and finally out of sight and back into court. Sometime later my Dad found out, and suggested I use the stock to wallpaper my room. It would serve as a reminder to invest in stocks that are proven and to get my investment advice from an authority who can be trused.

THE WISE INVESTMENT

The Scriptures are the best, most proven, and most authoritative "Investment Tip Sheet" you'll ever read. Like having a copy today of the *Wall Street Journal* that will be published forty years from now, the Bible tells you how to invest in your wife's self-esteem *today* if you want to experience a fabulous return in *forty years*. And, by the way, as her stock goes up, you share in the profits.

Your wife needs your creative investment energies if she is to become all that God created her to be. To help you in this area, here are some of the best investment tips I know of for giving both of you a return on your investment.

Investment Tip 1. Treat Her as a Participating Partner

Today the business world has all kinds of partnerships: silent partners, financial partners, equal partners, controlling partners, minority partners, and more. But in marriage, God intended for us to have only one kind: a fully participating partner.

The apostle Peter puts forth the concept of mutual partnership as he instructs a man to treat his wife as "a fellow-heir of the grace of life."[2] Although her function and role as a woman differs from yours as a man, she has an equal inheritance as a child of God. She is to be treated as a full partner in your life and marriage.

When you recognize your wife as a participating partner in your life, you give her value and build her esteem. If you exclude her from your life, you devalue her worth as a person, and her identity suffers. Without realizing it, you are sending to your wife an unmistakably clear signal: "I don't need you."

Some husbands believe the most difficult words to say are: "I love you," or "Will you forgive me?" But the three-word admission that seems the most threatening of all is: "I need you."

That *is* hard to admit, isn't it? When is the last time you told your wife you needed her? No, not just for this duty or that errand, but you really needed her — fully participating with you in life. When you express that need for her, she *feels* needed, because you become vulnerable and dependent upon her. She experiences her importance in your life.

But something in my male ego grabs hold of my tongue and keeps me from saying that to Barbara as often as I should. Pride? Yes. A false concept of manhood? Undoubtedly. But most assuredly, at the heart of the matter is foolishness. For I really *do* need my wife! She is God's personally hand-selected provision for my needs.

Some men fear they will lose their wife's respect by admitting their need. I've experienced quite the opposite. When I express my absolute need of Barbara, she is so built up and encouraged that she is free to respect me even more. I do not lose my identity as a man by expressing dependence on her.

You will make your wife a participating partner in your life when you look her in the face and say, "I need you." Why not make this an experiential reality in your marriage by frequently expressing:

- "I need you to listen as I talk about what's troubling me. And I need your perspective on the problem and your belief in me as a person."
- "I need you to help me become the man God made me to be."
- "I want you to have total access into my life. I need you to keep me honest in areas of my life in which I could stray from Christ. You may question me or confront me on any issue."
- "You are the person I most trust with my life."
- "I need you for your advice, judgments and wise counsel on decisions I face, especially at work."
- "I need your prayers for a temptation I am facing."

When I become the sole proprietor in our marriage and treat Barbara as a silent partner, we both lose. She loses the opportunities I can give to include her, develop her, and help her feel important. And I lose because I tend to make poor decisions when I am isolated from her.

So the investment tip is: "Let your wife in." Are you keeping her out of an area of your life? Do you tend to act independently of her in any area? Career or business? She may be more interested than you think. Financial matters? She needs to better understand them anyway. A difficult office relationship? Her advice might solve the problem.

As you make her a *full* participating partner, you express a valuable ingredient in building her self-image: trust. Ralph Waldo Emerson wrote, "Trust men and they will be true to you; treat them greatly and they will show themselves great."

Investment Tip 2. Protect Her

The apostle Peter also exhorts husbands, "You husbands likewise, live with your wives in an understanding way, as with a weaker vessel, since she is a woman."[3] Peter's emphasis here is on "understanding" because she is a "weaker vessel." Your wife wants a man who understands her and her needs.

Your wife needs to feel safe, secure and protected. As her husband, it's up to you to provide that security for her. I was reminded of a woman's need for protection years ago when I attended a couples conference. During the conference, a young woman was raped in her room. As the speaker warned the other conferees that a man had forced his way into this young woman's room, I noticed an interesting phenomenon. Instinctively, and in unison, as though led by an orchestra conductor, nearly every husband in the audience tenderly slid his arm around his wife. Likewise, almost every wife slipped closer under the protective arm of her husband. It was a physical gesture of a woman's need for safekeeping and a man's natural desire to protect his wife.

People use locks, burglar and fire alarms, and lighting systems to protect their possessions because they are valuable to them. When we invest in protecting our wives, we also are making a statement about their value to us, thus building their worth even more.

Certainly you already protect your wife physically. You wouldn't think of having it any other way. You discourage her from going out at night if it is dangerous. Or you protect her by encouraging her to lock the car when she goes shopping. You talk about what to do if a stranger forces his way into the house. And you provide the kind of locks and protection she needs at home for when you are away. All these statements and actions demonstrate that you want to protect her, that she indeed is valued, and that you care about what happens to her.

But are you protecting her from other muggers in her life, such as:

- Over-scheduling, letting her life get out of balance, and becoming driven?
- Others' manipulation of her emotions and life?
- Her own unrealistic goals or expectations, which set her up for failure?
- Her tendency to compare herself with others — where she repeatedly comes up short in her own eyes?
- Burnout at work?
- The children, who would take advantage of her weaknesses which they know so well?

- People who repeatedly discourage her?

Obviously, you can't protect your wife from every pressure, worry or fear, or from ever losing. But you can do your best to anticipate many of these problems before they occur and to establish a solid security system for her protection.

I can't explain the feeling, but I experience a satisfaction from protecting Barbara. Being firm and helping her say no causes me to feel that I'm really helping this woman be successful by protecting her from these outside forces. In fact, I think protecting her helps *my* self-image as a man as much as it does hers, because I feel needed and important.

One additional thought: Your wife will need different types of protection at different times in her life. As she goes

---

WIFE-BUILDER'S INVENTORY

The following questions help me "inventory" my most valuable friend, Barbara. By making myself answer these questions periodically, I maintain my protection of her and thus build her self-esteem.

- What is the pace of our life? Sometimes my schedule causes her more problems than it does me. Are there any breathers for her? For us?
- What kind of pace can she keep? For how long? What does she need after an intense period of time?
- What tends to crush her? What pops her balloon? What causes her to feel that she's failing? What can I do about it?
- What decisions do I need to make that will reduce pressure or bust a log jam? Am I putting off some things that, if I went ahead and did them, would facilitate her daily routine and thereby help her in the long run? (I've seen my procrastination cost Barbara a lot emotionally.)
- Does she need to be rescued for an evening? A weekend? An extended period? When can I carry her off for a romantic retreat for just us?
- What direction can I give her to protect her as she moves through a difficult period of time?

through various stages of adjustment she may need your protection and care even more than at other times.

Investment Tip 3. Honor Her

Here's an investment that will bring immediate value to your wife: honor. As in the case of a Medal of Honor being pinned on a soldier, or the Nobel Peace Prize being awarded, honor causes its recipient to be esteemed.

When God established marriage, He knew that one of the greatest components for building worth into another would be honor. We see this in His command to husbands, "Grant her honor as a fellow-heir of the grace of life."[4]

Webster defines honor as "high regard or great respect given; especially glory; fame; distinction." It is no wonder so many wives are flooding the workplaces today. Some have to work; they need the income. But some wives don't have to work; they work because they are seeking the honor, fulfillment and significance that they are not getting from their husbands.

Our love is kept fresh by understanding that the competition for Barbara is not over. Please don't misunderstand me — I'm not living in the daily fear that she's about to leave. But after watching the marriages of numerous Christian leaders disintegrate, I have come to some conclusions. One is that there is no such thing as a marriage blowout — only slow, small leaks. Like a tire that gradually has lost air without the driver noticing, many marriages have slowly gone flat.

Every marriage is susceptible to leaks, and ours is no exception. The world lures my wife with glittery, false promises of fulfillment and true significance. If I fail to honor her and esteem her as a woman of distinction, then I ignore the reality of her need and the alluring power of the world's promise. It's just a matter of time before she will begin to wear down and look elsewhere for worth. Sadly, in many cases today, women are finding what they've been missing, not in a career, but in another man's care.

So, in a healthy way, I still compete for my wife. The following are a few techniques to honor your wife that can give you a competitive edge while also building your wife's self-esteem.

Honor your wife by learning the art of putting her on a pedestal. If you will focus on honoring her and caring for her needs, and nurturing her as your most valued asset, then you can truly make a difference in how she feels about herself. Capture your wife's heart by treating her with respect, tenderness and the highest esteem.

One way to honor your wife is by by having compassion for her and by recognizing what she accomplishes. Frequently I look into Barbara's eyes and verbally express my wonder at all she does. She wears many hats and is an amazingly hard worker. At other times I stand back in awe of the woman of character she has become. Her steady walk with God is a constant stream of ministry to me.

Barbara's hats represent a challenge to her to be a winner in as many arenas as possible. But they are not just her hats; they're mine as well. Because I am to love her and care for her, then whatever brings pressure, fatigue, or failure to her is my concern, too.

Another way to bring honor to your wife is to speak to her with respect. Without careful attention, your tongue can become caustic, searing and accusing. Washington Irving once said, "The tongue is the only tool that gets sharper with use."

My tongue can be fueled by a disrespectful attitude. I work hard here. I'm not always as successful as I'd like, but I know honor begins with an attitude. Also, if any of the children ever talk back to Barbara or show disrespect, they know they have to deal with me when I get home from work. Our children are great, but they will mug her if I let them. She's outnumbered! So I encourage our children to respect her, too.

If your wife works outside the home, she has some unique needs in being honored. She may need the practical honor of a free evening once or twice a week when you volunteer to do it all: put the children to bed, clean the kitchen, do the laundry, etc.

Common courtesies are another way to honor your wife. You may think they were worthwhile only during courtship, but actually they are a great way to demonstrate respect and distinction now. Common courtesy is at the heart of servanthood; it says, "My life for yours." It bows before another to show esteem and dignity.

HATS A WIFE WEARS

Listed below are just a few of the hats some women wear today:

For the family:
  Meal planner
  Nurse
  Counselor/comforter
  Policeman and judge (to settle internal disputes)
  Clothier/wardrobe consultant
  Budget and financial planner/penny-pincher
  Teacher/tutor
  Cheerleader
  Career woman
  Spiritual advisor
  Nursery worker
  Seamstress
  Cook
  Maid
  Linguistics expert (specialist in the dialect of
    two-year-olds)
  Resident "Emily Post"
  Gardener
  Administrator/schedule planner
  Interior decorator
  Chauffeur
  Environmentalist (maintaining proper home
    environment)
  Family traditionalist
  Preserver of family history

For her husband:
  Confidante
  Companion
  Lover
  Advisor
  Encourager
  Partner
  Comforter
  Hostess and entertainer

For the community:
  Caring neighbor
  Gracious entertainer
  Volunteer
  Counselor
  Friend
  Church member

Imagine you have just received the following letter from your wife. How would you respond in writing? Be specific, and express how you feel.

My dearest husband. . .

Thank you for choosing me to share your life with you. Thank you for your honesty and transparency. I know it can be painful at times.

Deep down inside I really know that you love me. But I'm a woman and I need tangible reminders of your love. There is very little in this life of greater value to me than your love. I need it. I need you.

Could I ask a favor? I love to receive letters from you, but I don't ever want to ask for them . . . it takes all the fun out of receiving them if it's my idea. But would you write me a letter? I need to know:

- how you appreciate me . . .
- what I've done to show that I respect you . . .
- how I've been an encouragement to you . . .
- that you appreciate the "little things" I do every week for you . . .
- of your unconditional acceptance, just as I am (Is it there? I need to know) . . .
- how I am a partner with you . . .
- why you enjoy me . . .
- what you like about me . . .
- how I've changed for good or ways that you've seen me grow (I forget sometimes) . . .
- that you want to lead me and do what is best for me . . .
- that you want to meet my needs . . . and
- that your love *will* persevere.

You can write it any way you'd like, but please tell me. I really do respect you.

I love you,
Your wife

P.S. I'm not perfect either, but I'm glad we're in this thing together.

A woman is the crown jewel of God's creative handiwork. We should be careful not to treat her like one of the guys — slapping her on the back, for instance. The majesty of God is displayed in your wife. Why not exalt her by demonstrating courtesy? (Warning: If you suddenly begin a rash of "old courtesies," you may need to alert the cardiac care unit or get some smelling salts ready!)

This reminds me of a story my friend and Family Life Conference colleague Bob Horner told me:

> After noticing her neighbor bringing home flowers for his wife five nights in a row and passionately embracing her each time, Mrs. Richards brought this to her husband's attention. "You know, I've observed the strangest thing. Every evening this week our neighbor has walked to his door with a gift and a bundle of flowers and has given them to his wife as he kissed her and entered his home. Isn't that romantic? Why can't you do that?"
>
> Mr. Richards replied, "I couldn't do that. I hardly know her!"
>
> But as time passed, he began to think, *That must be what really excites women.* So he went out and bought a big box of candy and a bundle of his wife's favorite flowers. Arriving home a little early that afternoon, he rang the doorbell, and when his wife appeared, he passionately embraced her. As she fell in a heap on the floor, he exclaimed, "My gosh, what happened?"
>
> She answered, "Oh, this has been the worst day. Our son received a terrible report card, Mom was admitted to the hospital, the roast burned, the washing machine broke, and now to top it all off, you come home drunk!"

Sometimes our courtesy doesn't elicit the reaction we expect, but it's worth it.

I have found I can bring great dignity to Barbara by doing the following:

- Buying her a new dress, which *wasn't* on sale.
- Validating her emotions by listening before I answer.
- Appreciating her sexuality rather than make fun of her with comments such as, "Oh, you're just a woman!"
- Shopping with her and picking out something that I think she looks regal in.
- Giving her a free weekend while I stay home with the kids, so she can go antique shopping with friends.

Invest in your wife's self-image by finding your own creative ways to honor her. When you honor her, she'll become even more honorable. You both win!

**Investment Tip 4. Develop Her Gifts
and Horizons as a Woman**

Barbara's life is filled with battling the tyranny of the urgent, meeting needs, negotiating sibling rivalry disputes and juggling busy schedules. Most of her day is spent giving to others, and she generally ends it by dropping into bed, exhausted.

For years I watched her go through this daily ritual of giving her life away. Being the perceptive man that I am, it finally dawned on me that I had better help my favorite lady to express some of her creativity in other ways.

It occurred to me that while I'm taking management classes and reading professional journals, books and magazines, Barbara is occupied continually with the needs of our family. She needs me to look out for her and to encourage her to grow and develop, also.

The Scriptures mandate that I do this. Consider the familiar passage in Ephesians 5:25-29, especially: "He who loves his own wife loves himself; for no one ever hated his own flesh, but nourishes and cherishes it, just as Christ also does the church."

Notice the words describing what we are to do for our wives: love, nourish, cherish. All these are part of building into your wife's life and developing her self-esteem.

First, help her grow as a Christian. Your wife is your number one disciple. Do you encourage spiritual growth in your wife? It's the smartest thing you could possibly do. When your wife grows in this area, not only does she triumph at life, but *you* benefit as well. Help her grow spiritually by praying regularly for her and with her — at bedtime, in the morning before leaving for work, at meal times. You pick when, but pray. It *will* encourage her.

Interact together over God's Word and its application to your individual lives, as well as to your family. Encourage your wife to employ her spiritual gift in service to others outside your home if she has time.

Second, develop her talents. Take part in her life by nurturing the development of her talents that are dormant. Like fruit seeds that never have been planted in fertile soil and watered, your wife's gifts may need your care in order to germinate.

If you already have done this, you know she responds to this personalized focus. She feels that you value her and are helping her expand her life and utilize her gifts so that she might be even more productive as a person. Perhaps your wife already has influence. Can you apply additional resources so she can become even more effective?

Third, help her develop new horizons. Most of us fail to anticipate major change points in the lives of our wives, such as the birth of a child, children's teen years, menopause, and the empty nest. When your children leave home, your wife will suddenly have enormous chunks of time and attention to devote to another worthwhile cause. Are you developing her today so she will be ready to take some risks later?

Barbara is continuing to fashion a vision for her life that we both believe will be very satisfying to her. Why not assist your wife in uncovering a vision that will be meaningful to her? By helping her keep her horizons clear and focused in front of her, you will encourage her growth and development. And after years of helping her broaden her life, you will enjoy watching as your wife gains her own new sphere of influence.

Investment Tip 5. Assist in Problem Solving

Interesting, isn't it? Work gets our most creative problem-solving energies, best leadership, and most nobly controlled attitudes. Home usually gets the leftovers. One of my friends has on his office desk a plaque that reads: "Save a little for home."

No doubt, your wife would benefit if you saved more for home. Start by considering this question: What one problem in your wife's life, if solved, would truly strengthen her? Is there a complete roadblock in the way, or just a small boulder? How could you remove it?

If you are to see your wife win, you must be intimately involved in solving the problems that surround her life. If she is discouraged continually in certain situations, then put all your creative leadership ability behind her and gently give suggestions toward solving that problem. Here are some ideas:

- Watch your wife carefully. Observing her life may turn up problems that can be isolated and solved quickly.
- Get the facts. What exactly is the problem? Whose responsibility is it? What is the cause of the problem?
- Discuss your alternatives together. Be sure to find out what your wife really feels is best in the situation. She may be too close to the problem, or she may know what needs to be done and simply need your leadership and backing to make a decision.
- Go to God in prayer. Ask Him for the wisdom and the resources to solve the problem. Be careful of procrastinating; make a decision under God's leadership and then help your wife implement it.
- Evaluate the results. Inspect what happens. Refine the decision and its implementation through another thorough analysis of how things are working out.

A manager comes alongside his associate and applies resources to shore him up at the point of his weakness. You can, and should, do the same for your wife. It might mean you have to take some of her responsibilities. Does your wife have an area or two in which she consistently fails? Time management? Budgeting? Meal planning? Problem solving at work or at home? You can help. By choosing to develop her in these areas, you encourage her growth to handle the pressure. But you have a choice. Either develop her to handle responsibilities, or come alongside her yourself to help accomplish the tasks. She needs you to help her become all God made her to be.

Persevere With Your Investment

You may be married to a very insecure woman with a low self-esteem. And you may have tried already for a week or two to help her become more confident and self-assured, but because you haven't seen immediate results, you might be discouraged. Please don't give up. It may take years before you begin to see your wife blossom, but it is worth the effort and the wait. Don't quit.

One word of caution: You will be tempted to take the path of least resistance; that path will always be crowded with husbands. But you'll have great reward if you truly persist at investing your life in your wife.

King David understood the benefits of perseverance. When he first began to assemble and organize a group of men in the desert, he attracted "everyone who was in distress, and everyone who was in debt, and everyone who was discontented."[5] About four hundred of these vagabonds, social misfits and outcasts answered David's call for military training.

I'm realistic enough about leadership to know that David must have swallowed hard as he looked over this ragtag band. Undoubtedly he was tempted to put another advertisement in the paper and draft another group. But these were the men God gave him. So he accepted them and began to invest his life in theirs. He immediately started a program that would turn them into a band of trained soldiers. For more than seven years, David personally guided their development. Undoubtedly, progress was slow, setbacks were routine and improvement was, at times, unnoticeable.

Finally, after years of perseverance, there emerged a crack fighting unit of men who were experts with sword, sling, spear, and bow and arrows. In 1 Chronicles 11 we can read of the incredible feats these men achieved. Using them as the core of his militia, David drove all alien invaders out of Israel. And that group of misfits became known as David's "mighty men."[6]

Your wife couldn't possibly be described in such ragged terms as those men were, but her life and her self-esteem *can* become a trophy of the grace of God. If you will invest the time, energy and prayerful leadership needed to build into her life, she can become a more confident wife and woman.

BARBARA'S TIPS TO MEN

Barbara's tips on how to minister to a wife are also helpful:

- Seek to understand her role and her struggle. (If she works outside the home, understand her job and the pressures it places on her, especially regarding her role at home.)
- Verbalize often, especially in her times of failure and discouragement, your complete acceptance of her (be sure you really *do* accept her). Liberally verbalize belief in her as a person and in her ability and worth.
- Verbalize your need for her and back it up by sharing with her your fears, failures, needs, dreams, hopes and discouragements. Do it cautiously if this is new to you.
- Share at times when she can listen attentively and appreciate your transparency. (Don't share something serious when she's preoccupied with the kids or dinner.)
- Notice and praise her. Thank her for the things she does for you (meals, laundry, etc.).
- Be willing to help her work through difficulties in her life: discipline, problems with the children, relationships with friends and parents, fears, resentment, etc.
- Be patient and realize that building or rebuilding her self-esteem is a lifetime process. It is not static. Recaptured territory can be lost by giving up too soon.

In many ways I am a different woman from who I was on our wedding day. One of the most significant changes has been in my self-image. Dennis's willingness to listen and to change his schedule, and his consistent expression of praise for me, belief in me, and commitment to me have literally changed my life. There is hope. As you invest in your wife, I believe your reward in heaven will be great.

ESTEEM BUILDER PROJECT

(Use a sheet of paper if necessary.)

1. Which one of the following "investments" in your wife's life do you need to make a priority in the coming month?

    1. Treat her as a participating partner.
    2. Protect her.
    3. Honor her.
    4. Develop her gifts and horizons as a woman.
    5. Assist in problem solving.

2. Review the section in this chapter that best applies to your wife. Beside the investment you chose, list what action points you need to take. Write out your investment strategy and set your goals.

Three Secrets for Security

Secret 1. **Understand His Manhood**
Secret 2. **Respect His Person**
Secret 3. **Adapt to Him and His Dreams**

— 16 —
Securing Your Man

- The Collapsed Roof
- A Roof Is Like My Husband's Self-Esteem
- Choosing to Deny Yourself
- Understand His Manhood
- Give Him Total Acceptance
- Understand Our Male and Female Differentness
- Understand His Need For Work
- Understand His Sexual Need
- Benefits of Understanding
- Respect His Person
- Meet a Worthy Queen
- From the Palace of Persia to the Present
- Adapt to Him and Share His Dreams
- Esteem Builder Project

Woman to Woman: From Barbara

OUR CHILDREN AND I have been watching a new shopping center go up near our home. Initially, progress was rapid; the lot was cleared and the concrete pads were poured in one week. Then the walls went up, quickly followed by the framing for the roof.

But one day last week we turned the corner and slowed our van in disbelief. The entire structure had collapsed. The wooden roof trusses lay flat in neat rows, surrounded by the remains of the crumbled brick walls. It appeared there had been an explosion.

Puzzled, we inquired as to what had happened. We learned that the carpenters had failed to secure and brace the new structure properly. The building's roof had not been tied in and was supported in place only by two two-by-fours. It had collapsed in the middle of the day, under the weight of two carpenters.

As I reflected with amazement on the need for support in the building's structure, I saw a parallel in our marriage. The roof is like my husband's self-esteem. The Scripture teaches in Ephesians 5:23 that the husband is "the head of the wife as Christ also is the head of the church." When we first married, I committed to being under the roof of Dennis's protection. He had all the structural basics, but he was brand new at being my protector. Like that roof, he looked as though he were solidly in place, but he needed me to help *secure* him — to *brace* him by believing in him.

Fortunately, I did come alongside him. Through the years, the weight of life's various pressures has sometimes shaken him, but he has remained solidly over me as my roof, my protector. Today, though still not perfectly secure, my husband's structural integrity is much more stable. He tells me I have had a major part in helping him feel more sure of himself as a man and as a husband.

Likewise, you can strengthen your husband's self-esteem, but first you must recognize where he needs bolstering. Today many women are so caught up in finding their own identity that they, like those carpenters, make assumptions about their husband's self-confidence and security. Your mate may be full grown on the outside, but inside he undoubtedly feels some sense of insecurity. He's not so sure how to be a man in this world of women's growing independence and society's changing rules of relating.

But how does a wife build her husband's self-esteem? Basically, by making her responsibility as wife her number one focus. By developing the right attitude, a wife can meet her husband's deepest needs on the human level.

It has been said, "Behind every great man is a great woman."

One woman believed that literally. She and her husband, the mayor of a large city, were walking down a city street one day when a construction worker on a nearby scaffolding leaned over and shouted, "Hello, Peggy." She turned to look and recognized this fellow as an old boyfriend from high school.

She returned his greeting and they had a brief conversation before she and her husband continued their walk.

The mayor chuckled and said to his wife, "See there, if you had married him, you'd just be the wife of a construction worker."

She looked at him and said, "No, dear, if I'd married him, *he* would be the mayor of this city."

No matter what type of man you are married to, God wants you to set your sights on building his self-esteem. To help you begin, I recommend you do three things: (1) Gain an understanding of his manhood; (2) learn the secret of respecting his person; and (3) adapt to him and to his dreams.

---

1. Understand His Manhood

The book of Proverbs is probably my favorite book in the Bible because it contains such practical wisdom about everyday life. One of its main themes is the value of developing understanding.

> Incline your heart to understanding (2:2b).
> Understanding will watch over you (2:11b).
> Call understanding your intimate friend (7:4b).
> Wisdom rests in the heart of one who has understanding (14:3a).
> A man [or woman] of understanding walks straight (15:21b).
> Understanding is a fountain of life to him [or her] who has it (16:22a).

Notice that understanding is not an end in itself. It is a vehicle to wisdom, direction, and even to life. It enables you to feel for another person, to identify with his struggles and difficulties, and to know what to say and what not to say. In the husband-wife relationship, your level of understanding often determines your level of acceptance; however, total understanding is not necessary for the total acceptance which is crucial to building your husband's self-esteem.

At a recent Family Life Conference, I talked to more than a dozen women who were experiencing problems in their marriages. One woman resented her husband's schedule. Another disagreed with her husband regarding the handling of their

children. A third was a young woman whose fiancé was jealous
of the time she spent with her sister.

My advice to all these women was basically the same:
Seek to understand *why* your husband or fiancé is feeling or
acting this way. Focus on *him*, not on the negative circumstances
and how *you* are affected. Is he communicating by his action
some deep needs for affirmation, commitment or loyalty?

Also, give him your complete acceptance, even if you
don't understand totally. It may be necessary to ask God to
help you accept your husband, for your situation may not be
easy to live with.

Why is acceptance so important to a man? Without it,
he will feel you are pressuring him to become something he's
not. With it, he will sense you love him for what he is today
and not for what you hope he will become.

Understand Differentness

There are three areas in which most wives have difficulty
understanding their husbands. These three are foundational to
all men, and having knowledge of them is essential if you are
to build your husband's self-esteem.

The first is understanding male and female differentness.
We are being taught today that men and women are just two
"sexually interchangeable units." To aid woman's quest for
political and economic equality with man, many experts have
sought to explain away all social, emotional and intellectual
differences. These educators, sociologists and psychologists
imply that there are no differences between men and women
other than the obvious biological ones.

As a result, we wives have been deceived into thinking
our husbands are basically like us. Men, as well as women,
have lost their sense of wonder and appreciation for our God-
given maleness and femaleness. This tainted perspective clouds
our perceptions of our husbands.

Without a true understanding of how God has made our
husbands different, we will be tempted to resent them for being
"the way they are." If we resent our husbands, we are ultimately
resenting God for His design of their manhood.

I have found that as I increase in understanding my
husband's distinctions as a man, I am less likely to be critical
of potential irritants. My understanding quotient took a giant

stride forward when I read Dr. Joyce Brothers's book, *What Every Woman Should Know About Men*.

In her book, Dr. Brothers confessed she was astounded to find the differences between men and women to be so vast. She devotes an entire chapter to the differences between men's and women's brains. She cites repeated evidence to prove that, although male and female brains are made up of two basic parts, a left and a right hemisphere, the function for each sex is quite different.

Simply put, a man's brain operates specifically, while a woman's operates wholistically. The right hemisphere of a man's brain can and does operate without the left being involved, and vice versa. A woman's brain uses and integrates both hemispheres simultaneously. Thus, a man can give more focused attention to his work or project, while his wife can be tuned in to everything around her. This makes her more perceptive of people and their feelings than her husband is, and it enables her, especially if she is a mother, to know what is going on in every part of the house at once.[1]

I now understand why Dennis can be reading the paper and not know that the children, a few feet away, are terrorizing one another. Rather than get angry with him for his apparent non-involvement, I realize that one side of his brain is "off" and that he's just being himself, a man.

Also, when he comes home from work, the children sometimes scream for his attention, yet he doesn't seem to hear them. I tell them, "Relax, kids, your daddy's not home yet!"

Exasperated, they reply, "Yes he is, Mom. He's standing right here."

But I tell them, "*We* know he's home, but *he* doesn't know it yet!"

Dennis needs me to help him tune in at home. We both know it. In the first incident above, I may go into the living room, tap him on the shoulder and ask him to solve the problem. Or I may do it myself. But because of this new understanding of his masculinity, I'm better able to accept him and his differentness. The effect of his feeling accepted is a greater freedom to be himself and a growing resolve to learn and change.

The beauty of understanding male and female differentness is seeing more clearly God's detailed design in the two sexes. He did not create man as more important than woman. He values them equally. But in order to reflect more accurately the Trinity to the unbelieving world, God wisely designed us each, man and woman, with built-in distinctions for the purpose of fulfilling different responsibilities in marriage. In the living out of these biblical patterns, not only do we reflect God's image, but both partners also experience the contentment intended in marriage.

Understand His Need for Work

A second area of struggle for many wives is the husband's job and its pressures.

The past three decades of the new ideologies about women's rights have left Christian women in a wake of confusion. We have been told to seek personal fulfillment at the expense of husband and children, if necessary. Family, we hear, should not stand in the way of self.

Consequently, many of us Christian wives have lost sight of our husbands' needs as we have focused intently on our own. Even though over 50 percent of you reading this book are working outside the home, I'd like to explain briefly the importance of work in your husband's life.

Man was given responsibility by God to toil, sweat, and gain from the labor of his hands. A man's work is part of the ruling and managing purpose that God spoke of in Genesis 1:26: "Let them rule over the fish of the sea and over the birds of the sky and over the cattle and over all the earth."

Your husband needs work in order to realize the satisfaction inherent in executing God's stated purpose of ruling and managing God's creation. His work gives him a sense of significance and importance in the world as he sees his efforts affecting life in the present and in the future for good.

But this drive for significance sometimes pushes a man to extremes. In his effort to gain a sense of well-being and significance, he often becomes enslaved to his job. Attempting to gain importance through wealth or position, he makes his work his god. For hundreds of years, men have confused their net worth with their self-worth.

On the other hand, a man who doesn't work lacks true self-respect. In this age of workaholism, losing a job is a traumatic blow to a man's esteem. It strikes at the core of his dignity. A man who doesn't work can't enjoy the satisfaction of a solid day's productivity.

Your husband needs you to help him keep these two extremes in balance. He needs you to praise him for his work, but not to push him to gain too much too quickly.

When a man loses or quits his job, his self-esteem sinks. In these times, he needs you to stand beside him and encourage his efforts at finding employment. Offer to type his resumé, and make it first class. With his permission, call a few friends in your church who might know of jobs. Pray for him that God will lead him to a job where he can utilize his strengths and make his own contribution.

What if he is employed, but you don't like his job? What if you think he spends too much time there? Do you still support him? Won't that only encourage him to work more?

Ann Landers received a letter over twenty years ago from a woman who was lonely and jealous of the time her husband spent at a local diner. She printed the letter with this response, "When you begin to offer the same thing on the menu at home, he may spend his time there."

The point of Ann's response is to make yourself more attractive to your husband than his acquaintances and job. Nagging won't bring him home. But understanding your husband's need for work and genuinely praising him will make you more attractive to him. He may find he wants to spend more time with you and less at work, because his work can't fulfill his need for companionship.

Understand His Sexual Need

The third sphere we wives, for the most part, do not really understand is how our husband's self-image is vitally linked to his sexuality. Sometimes, we women judge our husband's sexual needs by our own.

Many Christian wives express being offended because their husbands are sexual creatures. This attitude communicates rejection to a man. To ignore his sexual needs, to resist his initiation of sex, or merely to tolerate him, is to tear at the heart of his self-esteem.

Jill Renich points this out in her book, *To Have and To Hold*. She states that for a man, "Sex is the most meaningful demonstration of love and self-worth. It is a part of his own deepest person."[2]

Dr. Joyce Brothers sheds further light on men and their need for sex when she writes, "By and large, men are far more apprehensive when it comes to sex than a woman might believe."[3] Those statements seem contrary to popular belief, don't they? Modern men are portrayed via the media as always confident and assertive sexually.

The truth is, the typical man worries a lot. He worries about his performance, his wife's enjoyment, and his ability to satisfy her. He worries about the future and all those tales he's heard about losing his ability to make love. This worry is a sign of low self-confidence. Thus, a man who feels like a failure in the marriage bed will seldom have the deep, abiding self-respect for which he longs.

But, as Jill Renich writes, "To receive him with joy, and to share sexual pleasure builds into him a sense of being worthy, desirable and acceptable."[4]

Talk freely with your husband about this area of your relationship. Tell him of your fears, your worries, your misconceptions. Allow him to rescue you from these as you talk together of the truth. But don't tell him if you're only making an excuse for why you won't change. If you aren't willing to risk change, you leave him vulnerable to having his needs met elsewhere.

But what if your husband expresses little sexual need? Are you naively content because that means less risk for you? Or are you accepting or even resentful of his indifference without seeking to understand why?

Dr. Brothers addresses this issue as well. She calls it sexual boredom — complacency in the bedroom. She writes,

Sexual boredom is a major element in the 'twenty-year fractures,' those divorces that occur after the children are grown and husband and wife find themselves alone for the first time in years. If sex got lost in the shuffle of child-rearing and career-building, and if a man meets a younger woman who finds him attractive, he is extremely vulnerable. Not only because of his boredom and the difficulty of adjusting to life as a twosome again, but also because he is in the time in his life when change for change's sake looks good to him anyway. Too many women accept their husbands' decreasing interest in sex without stopping to think what might be causing it."[5]

Your husband may lack an interest in his sexual relationship with you for one of several reasons:

- He may be too busy. Many workaholics have nothing left over for home.
- He may be burying his sex drive, along with many other emotions. You or a good Christian counselor need to begin to help him open up.
- He may be experiencing depression, which takes away other basic drives as well.
- He may be deeply afraid of further rejection if you have in any way communicated rejection in the past.
- Unfortunately, he may be involved with another woman.

Women are generally security-minded, but too often a woman's need for security leads her into a sexual rut. Her husband may not say much, so she assumes he is satisfied, too. But he may not be. Beware of complacency. Be willing to make some personal sacrifice to protect your marriage from sexual boredom.

Great sacrifice communicates great love. Freely giving of yourself to your mate will make you a magnet to him, drawing him home, keeping him safe. The wife who really loves her husband will choose to take risks to please her man.

As you spend time together physically, be sure to reassure your husband verbally of your unconditional acceptance of him, especially if he is insecure in this area. Tell him you like his body and that his imperfections and mistakes don't matter to you. His confidence will grow if you allow him the freedom to be himself and to be imperfect.

To please your husband sexually is to build his sense of value as a man. He will feel needed, fulfilled and confident. He will experience the protection that marriage was intended to provide from the temptations of the world.

Benefits of Understanding

Understanding your husband and his differentness, his need for work, and his sexuality will enable you to accept him more readily.

The more you understand him, the more you will be able to:

- help him put life in its proper context when he gets down on himself;
- help him comprehend his own humanity, failures and frailties;
- help him open up (by creating an environment that enables him to be real with you);
- help him learn to laugh at his weaknesses and at the aging process (by laughing with him, but never at him);
- help him see his positive progress by reminding him how far he has already come.

Understanding Him Makes You Valuable

As you gain understanding and give acceptance, your mate will develop the confidence to be vulnerable emotionally. He will feel freer to express fear, sadness, anger and affection. You will become his most valuable asset and he will treasure you, trust you and depend on you.

You will experience the truth of Proverbs 14:1: "The wise woman builds her house, but the foolish tears it down with her own hands."

---

2. Respect His Person

Part of God's specific instruction to wives is found in Ephesians 5:33b: "Let the wife see to it that she respect her husband." In the Amplified Bible this verse reads, "And let the wife see that she respects and reverences her husband — that she notices him, regards him, honors him, prefers him, venerates and esteems him; and that she defers to him, praises him, and loves and admires him exceedingly."

Why does God focus on this quality of respect? Why didn't He select other positive and necessary traits, such as kindness, sympathy, or forgiveness? Why not an emphasis for wives on love?

I believe that God, as the designer of men, knew they would be built up as they are respected by their wives. When a wife respects her husband, he feels it — is supported by it — and is strengthened from it.

Your husband wants and needs to make a contribution in life that is worthy of another's respect. He needs to know you feel he is important. Without your respect, he can't respect himself. You are his mirror. When you express your respect, he feels valuable and esteemed. You have further secured his self-image.

Meet a Worthy Queen

The Old Testament contains a wonderful story about a marriage of great respect. It's like a fairy tale come true. The book of Esther tells of a celebration given by King Ahasuerus (or Xerxes), ruler of the Persian empire. As a grand finale to the rejoicing, the king gave a generous banquet for all the people in the capital city of Susa. He called for his queen, Vashti, to come "with her royal crown in order to display her beauty to the people and the princes, for she was beautiful" (1:11). But Queen Vashti refused.

Instead of honoring his request, Queen Vashti acted with "contempt" (verses 17,18). She embarrassed her husband publicly before the entire population of the capital city. So, according to the custom of the times, she was removed from her position of honor. The search began for a new queen, one who would be more worthy.

Esther was selected from among the most beautiful women of the kingdom to be the new queen. As the story continues, we discover that Esther was more than a beautiful young woman. Her worthy character is revealed as the romantic tale suddenly changes to a drama.

Queen Esther is informed by her uncle of a plot to destroy all the Jews living in the kingdom. Uncle Mordecai urges Esther to go to the king and plead with him on behalf of her people. The young queen is faced with a tough decision. She knows that the rules and the laws of the palace dictate that no one can approach the king without being summoned (4:11), and she knows what happened to the queen before her. But she was willing to risk her position for a higher good (4:14-16).

In her decision to approach him, several things are apparent about her relationship with her husband the king. First, she was not presumptuous. She came before him as his queen, wearing her royal robes, but she came humbly and she stood and waited (5:1). She didn't barge into the throne room. Even though she had a relationship with the king, she didn't abuse that privilege. And God honored her. When the king saw her standing in the entrance, he called her in and willingly received her. Esther was wise in her timing and respectful in her attitude.

Second, she respected her husband and his position as king. As she reached the throne, she touched his golden scepter, showing she recognized his authority and power.

Esther never let her respect slip. She didn't dump all the facts on him and overwhelm him as soon as she was in his presence. She exhibited her high regard for her husband twice before she ever said a word.

Third, Esther began her reply to her husband, "If it please the king . . . " (5:4). In the other two recorded conversations between this king and queen, the same statement prefaces her remarks. This was *not* just an official formality, but a genuine expression to Ahasuerus of her overall commitment, respect and submission to him as her husband and her authority.

Over the years in our marriage, there have been many difficult subjects I felt needed to be brought to Dennis's attention. I wasn't sure exactly what to say. At times, I was fearful of his response. But somewhere along the way I learned what Queen Esther knew about broaching hot topics in marriage.

I learned to wait patiently for an appropriate time. I also discovered the importance of prefacing my comments with statements like these:

"I have something I need to talk to you about; would this be a good time?"

"I want you to know I love you and I'm committed to you and I believe in you."

"I may be wrong, and if I am, I want you to tell me, but I feel . . ." or "I sense that . . ."

What I try to do, and I believe Esther did as well, is assure Dennis of my respectful loyalty to him as my partner and authority before I present my case. There are times when I speak frankly about his weaknesses and how I'm affected, but he is much more able to hear because of my loyalty and verbal reassurances. He knows that even if nothing changes, I will still remain committed to him.

From the Palace of Persia to the Present

As wives, we do not need to attain royalty to become like Queen Esther. A jeweled crown and a royal robe did not make her a true queen; her attitude did. Esther shows us the importance of being a perceptive student of our own husbands. She knew hers well. She acknowledged his position and authority and chose to give him honor, praise and esteem.

Life has changed from Esther's day, but a wife's respect for her husband is still essential. Every husband has been given authority by God. Whether your mate's realm is a tiny one or a large one, he desperately needs your respect for who he is and what he does. By freely giving him this respect, you affirm him at the very core of his being. He feels proud to be a man. His self-esteem is more firmly established on a solid foundation.

Perhaps you are thinking, "But I see little, if anything, to respect." Perhaps you are like the young mother I know whose husband drank heavily and spent little time with the children. She had a difficult time viewing him with respect and honor. A deliberate change of focus from his weaknesses to his few strengths enabled her to see her mate in a positive light. Gaining a better perspective may aid you in esteeming your husband, too.

When photographing an extensive landscape, it's impossible to focus simultaneously on the flowers in the foreground and the mountains in the background. So the photographer adjusts the camera lens to bring his chosen area of interest into focus. When the photograph is developed, even the weeds in the field look good in the context of the overall picture.

Similarly, in viewing your husband, you must choose your focus. Continually looking at his flaws will affect your overall perception of him negatively. Yet, you can blur the image of those weaknesses so that you hardly notice them at all, and you can focus sharply on the positive qualities, causing genuine respect to develop.

The Scripture says, "Whatever is true, whatever is honorable, whatever is right, whatever is pure, whatever is lovely, whatever is of good repute, if there is any excellence and if anything worthy of praise, let your mind dwell on these things" (Philippians 4:8,9). Give attention to the things in your husband that are admirable, rather than to those that are negative. You can then offer him the respect that will build his self-esteem.

3. Adapt to Him and His Dreams

The chameleon is noted for its ability to change color to blend in with its environment. This capacity is the creature's primary means of protection. A chameleon can be viewed in two ways. First, we might despise it for its lack of character. After all, anyone who changes that readily must not know what he wants to be. To change constantly to match one's environment could be seen as being wishy-washy and spineless with no constant identity of his own.

Or we could see this four-footed creature as wise. He doesn't lose his identity as a chameleon when he switches from green to brown. He is only protecting himself from potential danger and harm. Viewed positively, this lowly reptile becomes clever, creative and competent.

Of course, the chameleon doesn't have the choice we women do regarding adapting. He has no free will. He instinctively does what he was created to do. He illustrates that adapting to our husbands is more than a "how-to" question — it's a matter of perspective as well.

Leonard Bernstein, the famous orchestra conductor, was once asked, "What is the most difficult instrument to play?"

CHARACTER INVENTORY

What are your husband's positive character qualities? Is he compassionate, kind and sensitive toward people? Is he disciplined and dedicated? Is he faithful and loyal, persevering in difficulties? Do the words truthful, honest or decisive describe your mate? What are his talents and strengths? Make a list. Refresh your memory. Refurbish your respect.

List at least five positive character qualities that you respect and admire in your husband.

1. _____

2. _____

3. _____

4. _____

5. _____

He replied, "Second fiddle. I can get plenty of first violinists, but to find one who plays second violin with as much enthusiasm, or second French horn, or second flute, that's a problem. And yet if no one plays second, we have no *harmony.*"

Creating a harmony in your marriage necessitates adapting. To adapt means to acclimate, naturalize, become accustomed to, or become familiar with. When a woman adapts to her husband, she does not lose her identity, as some would say. Instead, she broadens it. In giving she isn't depleted, but *expanded,* just as the second violin enriches the music of the first violin.

Adapting is being a helpmate, not a help-maid. It's being a complement to your husband and not a competitor. Your position as helper was not designed by God to be an inferior one. Have you noticed that in the New Testament Jesus referred to the Holy Spirit as the "Helper"? That title doesn't make Him a lesser member of the Trinity. God also refers to Himself as a helper in other passages (Psalms 54:4; 30:10; 33:20). The term "helper" identifies His role; it describes His relationship with man.

Likewise, the role of wife is no less significant than that of husband. The terms used to describe our function merely tell us *how* we should relate to our mates. They have nothing to do with our value as women.

It is a special calling to come alongside a man, to adapt to him, and to help him become all that God intended. It is a privilege that should not be demeaned. Be an involved partner in your marriage. Speak your convictions, opinions and ideas. In order to lead your family intelligently, your husband needs your input. But maintain the delicate balance of being a helpmate without usurping his leadership. Adapting to your husband grants him the freedom to lead you and your family, and makes it easier for him to follow God.

Share His Dreams

Through the years, as I have tried to fulfill my role as wife, I at times have struggled with the feeling that my desires and dreams were getting lost in the shuffle. Adapting to, respecting and even understanding my husband have been difficult on many occasions. Sometimes the sacrifice seemed too great. In these instances, I felt as if God were leading me where I hadn't chosen to go and where I was not skilled, because of His will for Dennis.

During those times, the following beliefs have enabled me to maintain the right positive perspective and see my situation more clearly.

1. I believe firmly in God's sovereignty and am sure of His loving direction for my life.
2. I believe God sovereignly led me to marriage. As a result, I have chosen to submit my life not only to God's authority, but to my husband's as well.
3. I am convinced God is still sovereignly leading me through my marriage, just as much as when I was single. God's will for me is not hampered by my married state.
4. While much of God's will for me is a consequence of His will for Dennis, I believe I'm not a tag-along or an appendage. We are partners; we are one. God's will for *him* is God's will for *me*.

Maybe your husband has dreams of other ways he would like to use his life and abilities. Do you know what they are? Does he feel free to talk to you about new ideas? Or do you ignore or discount his thoughts because you don't like them, or because they would require you to give up some of your goals, or because you feel they were impossible anyway? Perhaps you were afraid of what it would cost you for him to accomplish his dream (a move, your career, loss of friends, further financial risk, time pressures, etc.).

Proverbs 20:5 says, "A plan in the heart of a man is like deep water, but a man [woman] of understanding draws it out." Do you know what plans or dreams or visions lie in the heart of your husband?

A man who feels free to share the depths of his heart with his wife, knowing she will listen without criticizing him, and knowing she is willing to adapt to whatever he wants to do with his life, is a man who is free to become all God intended and to do all God has planned.

It Takes Years for Him to Become a Man

It's been six months since that small shopping center near our home began to rise out of the ground. It's near completion in spite of its early setback. There have been changes and structural modifications. Some were external, obvious to us as we passed by. Other structural improvements were made but they were internal and couldn't be seen.

Your husband, like that shopping center, is still under construction. His self-esteem will take time, modifications and improvements. Internally your attitude of acceptance, respect and adapting are all essential to his structural integrity as a man. Your external behavior matters too, for your words and actions *can* help construct a secure man.

Remember, it takes years for a man to become a strong husband. Be patient with him. Put aside your high expectations of how the phantom husband would lead his family spiritually, or behave socially, or perform intellectually. Keep your hope in God, not in your man. Then you will not be disappointed.

ESTEEM BUILDER PROJECT
(Use a sheet of paper if necessary.)

1. Which of these attitudes are most difficult for you to have toward your husband?
   _____ 1. Understanding his manhood
   _____ 2. Understanding his need for work
   _____ 3. Understanding his sexual need
   _____ 4. Giving him respect
   _____ 5. Adapting to him
   _____ 6. Sharing his dreams
2. List three reasons.
   _____
   _____
   _____

3. What can you do about this problem area? Pray? Change your focus? Other? _____
   _____
   _____

4. What are your husband's dreams and goals? List as many as you can think of. Then ask him one evening to look at your list and see how on target you are.

5. Ask yourself: Am I really willing for him to become and do all that God has planned? What do I fear most? A move (near or far)? A change in our finances? The position I would be expected to fill as a result of my husbands's position? In prayer, give that area of fear and insecurity to God. Ask Him to free you from that personal concern so you will not be a hindrance to God's plan for your husband's life, but a true biblical helper.

— 17 —
Keep Your Torch Burning

- The Twenty-Kilometer Walk
- Perseverance and Change
- Perseverance and Progress
- Perseverance and Purpose

OUR GOOD FRIEND Mary Graham told us this stirring story which she watched unfold during the 1984 Olympics in Los Angeles.

With the Coliseum filled to the brim and the world looking on, the twenty-kilometer walk began. Hardly comparing with Edwin Moses's efforts to remain undefeated, and with Carl Lewis's four gold medals, the event began with about fifty entrants. They were to take seven laps inside the Coliseum, then exit the quarter-mile track and walk their race on the streets of Los Angeles for the next two and a half hours.

With only three laps completed, the walker from El Salvador began to trail the other entrants by a great distance. On the fourth lap, he was passed by all the other participants in the race. And as the other entrants exited the stadium en masse after completing their seventh lap, the bronzed young man still had two laps to go. The crowd cheered him on, however, and as he passed each section in the stands, they chanted, "El Salvador! El Salvador!" Finally he exited the Coliseum.

Two and one-half hours later, the pack of walkers re-entered the Coliseum, and of course, one emerged as the victor. He was given his gold medal and crowned with a sombrero as the crowd warmly applauded his achievement.

The crowd then settled back for the 10,000-meter run. Twenty minutes into that race, the twenty contestants were joined on the track by another man — the walker from El Salvador. The crowd roared with approval as he walked around the oval track, avoiding the runners of the race then in progress.

Then the crowd rose to its feet when another walker entered the stadium course. The determined walker from Central America, two laps behind when he left the Coliseum, had passed this other walker on the course! In unison, more than 100,000 people chanted "El Salvador! El Salvador!" as the young man finished the race — and collapsed.

The trauma wagon rushed to his side, but instead of taking the young walker directly through the exit where it had taken other exhausted athletes, the driver took a "victory lap" for that young Olympian. The crowd went wild. They cheered and applauded the courageous man whose name they didn't even know. It didn't matter who had won the race; the young man from El Salvador had persisted and finished.

In a similar way, God has given us a course in life. We must run in such a way that we are able to endure, that we are able to finish the race that is set before us.

The book of Hebrews gives us a sober challenge: "Therefore, since we have so great a cloud of witnesses surrounding us, let us also lay aside every encumbrance, and the sin which so easily entangles us, and let us run with endurance the race that is set before us, fixing our eyes on Jesus, the author and perfecter of faith, who for the joy set before Him endured the cross, despising the shame, and has sat down at the right hand of the throne of God. For consider Him who has endured such hostility by sinners against Himself, so that you may not grow weary and lose heart."[1]

Look to Christ when attempting to build into your mate. He will not disappoint you. He *does* answer prayer. He *is* at work in your mate. He *does* know what He is doing. Trust Him and keep growing strong in Him. Without Jesus Christ, no one can persevere in running the race. He is our hope.

Perseverance and Change

As you tenaciously work to elevate your mate's self-esteem, don't expect change to occur overnight. A Chinese proverb states, "A journey of a thousand miles begins with a single step." Lasting change rarely occurs immediately, but it can occur as you are faithful to do what is right.

Be careful about setting your expectations too high. Circumstances change, as do people. The process may be like climbing in the Rockies — you climb one foothill, only to find another mountain staring you in the face. That's the nature of life. But you will make little progress in your marriage apart from your total commitment. We encourage you to keep climbing.

At our Family Life Conferences, we like to ask people, "If you had five frogs on a log and three of them decided to jump, how many frogs would you have left on the log?"

The answer is: five.

There are five frogs on the log because there is a difference between *deciding to jump* and *jumping*. Commitment was never meant to be divorced from action.

As you've read these pages, you may have seen a couple of strategies you should have implemented, but you haven't done it. They seem too risky. But commitment demands risk, and risk builds trust and faith in your relationship with God. Why not exercise that muscle and "jump"?

Perseverance and Progress

Your mate's self-image, as well as yours, is progressive. That means you both are in process. It takes time. A lifetime. Paul writes, "But we all, with unveiled face beholding as in a mirror the glory of the Lord, *are being transformed* into the same image . . ."(italics added).[2] God is at work. We won't see the finished product until we stand before Him and see Him face to face, but we are being transformed into the likeness of His image.

And that process benefits others, as well as you. Your children need to see a harmonious marriage modeled by their parents. They need to see the two of you, imperfect people who are vessels of God's perfect love, keep going after you fail. They need to learn from your example.

As your children see both of you growing in your own self-esteem, they will experience more security and will develop in their self-image, too. Importantly, they will be able to obey and follow Christ throughout their lifetimes without being imprisoned by their own feelings of inadequacy and insecurity.

The world also benefits from your example. It is in the process of perishing. But you are the salt and light of the world to your next-door neighbors, associates at work, family members, and friends.[3] For them, your marriage may be the brightest reflection of what God is like. In fact, as we move into the twenty-first century, your marriage could become one of the greatest witnessing tools in our society.

Perseverance and Purpose

Finally, as you run the race, keep your direction and vision clear. Since you are partners for life, moving together toward a common goal, you can endure the race. As a couple, lose yourself in the infectious person of Jesus Christ and your love for Him. Cut yourself loose from the world and all of its alluring trappings, and grab hold of the imperishable will of God.

Also, as a couple, invest your lives in others. Teach them how to build up their mate's self-esteem. Instruct them to leave a heritage that will outlive them. The Great Commission of Jesus Christ is still the greatest cause with which the world has ever been presented. Go. Preach. Teach. Share Christ with all who will listen.

Who knows, someday when you are whisked away to heaven, you may meet a throng of angels, saints and friends who have been cheering you on as you ran the race with your mate here on earth. Their applause, along with the nodding approval of Him who knows all, will tell you your faithfulness was not in vain.

For information on other books and tapes by the same authors, write us:
Dennis and Barbara Rainey
P.O. Box 23840
Little Rock, AR 72221

Appendix

How to Know God

The tragic 1985 earthquake in Mexico City took hundreds of lives, but in the midst of the rubble and ruin there were countless stories of how people had been miraculously rescued. One such rescue was that of Ruben Vera Rodriguez, a 38-year-old filing clerk who was buried beneath four floors of debris for almost four days.

"His ordeal began at 7:18 A.M. on Thursday, when the first shock wave washed across the city. He was working on the third floor of one of the Labor and Social Welfare Ministry buildings.

"The walls buckled, the pillars dissolved and the four floors above him crashed down. He fell to the floor. The ceiling came to a halt 1 1/2 feet above the inclined floor. He had landed with his head down, his feet up. 'I couldn't move one foot,' he says. 'I couldn't raise my arm. I was buried alive.'

"Vera Rodriguez heard other office workers crying for help, and the sound of rubble being moved. He felt he would be rescued quickly, but two days passed with no help. The voices of his colleagues fell silent.

"From the first day of his entrapment, he had seen light from above reflected in front of him. So, gashing his flesh, he wriggled his way backward toward the light. Steadily, painfully, he crawled up toward the roof. Every so often he stopped and tried to gather his energy for another effort.

"When the light would dim, he knew that it was getting dark. But he continued to crawl. He was about ten feet from the opening when his progress was blocked by a concrete slab and a steel bar. He yelled, "Here, up here! Help me! Please! " 'The rescuers were stunned. I was alive. . . .' After about an hour of digging, he was freed. 'I felt I had emerged from the womb. The workers joked about how I was born once again, given new life. And it was true.' "[1]

Like Vera Rodriguez, you may feel trapped. Trapped under the rubble of a life that has ignored what God and His Word have to say about how to live.

You may have lived a religious life, but somehow your religion has not provided the fulfillment and satisfaction you feel it should — something is missing and you feel trapped.

Or maybe you find yourself trapped in a marriage that is less than the best and you have turned to this book for solutions, thinking, "God may have some solutions for my life after all."

Perhaps you've seen everything you touch "turn to gold" and yet you also feel trapped by "things" that just haven't satisfied as you had hoped they would.

Or perhaps you compare yourself with a friend who calls himself a "Christian." Your friend is different. Life doesn't box him in; he isn't under the pile; and he seems able to deal with life's difficulties with a perspective that is not the same as yours.

No matter what makes you feel trapped, you must be seeking to be who God made you to be as a person or you wouldn't be reading this book. And maybe in the process of reading our book you've become aware that in order to build into your mate's life, you need to be closer to God than you presently are. In fact, you may have realized that you need God in your life, period. You need to know God personally.

If you've come to this conclusion, then you are very close to being "rescued" and truly "born again," but in a way much different from that of Vera Rodriguez. Let us explain how that can happen.

The Reality

One of the greatest realities the Scriptures teach is that of God's love for each person. Look at these statements:

You are honored and I love you (Isaiah 43:4b).
I have loved you with an everlasting love; therefore

I have drawn you with loving-kindness (Jeremiah 31:3b).
"I have loved you," says the Lord (Malachi 1:2a).

God's love for us is made obvious throughout the Bible, and it is also apparent that He desires us to live a significant and rewarding life. Jesus said, "I came that they might have life, and might have it abundantly" (John 10:10b).

Since it is true that God loves us, and that He desires that we experience His ultimate purpose for our lives, then why is it that many today do not experience God's love and the life He offers? And since God *wants* a relationship with every individual, then why doesn't everyone automatically have it?

What separates people from the love of God today?

The Rubble

In the first moments after the walls had crumbled and the dust had settled, Vera Rodriguez did not fully understand the seriousness of his predicament. He didn't immediately realize he was helplessly trapped under four stories of twisted steel and concrete. After waiting for two days for help to come to him, he began to labor tirelessly for two more days trying to save himself. Though he had moved closer and closer to the light, he eventually discovered an insurmountable obstacle between himself and freedom, barring the path to life and trapping him in certain death.

Similarly, man finds himself helplessly trapped under the rubble of a life lived for himself. Isaiah wrote of this self-centered attitude: "All of us like sheep have gone astray, each of us has turned to his own way" (Isaiah 53:6a).

Ignoring God, either by outright rejection of God and His ways or by simply never bothering to pay attention to what He has to say, we choose to go our "own way." The result of both attitudes is the same: separation from God. Consider the following:

For all have sinned and fall short of the glory of God (Romans 3:23).

The word *sin* may bring to your mind lists of rules that prohibit. But the word actually comes from a Greek archery term used to measure the distance between the bull's eye and where the archer's arrow hit. That distance was called the "sin." It literally was a measurement of how far the archer had missed the mark. The "bull's eye" for humanity is God's perfect character. The Bible speaks of His character as holy, blameless and righteous. He is the one in whom there is no flaw or imperfection. Against this perfect standard, exemplified by Christ's life, each person must measure his or her own life. As each person measures himself against God's perfect ideal, he realizes he misses the mark. Not just once, but repeatedly, man falls short.

Realizing their imperfection, many begin to labor tirelessly to make themselves "acceptable to God." Yet their efforts are futile: Sin's barrier creates a humanly insurmountable obstacle between them and God. Just as Vera Rodriguez found a slab of concrete and steel blocking his escape route, so we, too, find that our sin and imperfect nature form an impenetrable blockade between us and God. No amount of human "good works" or "religious efforts" can remove the consequences of sin.

The result of sin is seen in Romans 6:23: "For the wages of sin is death." *Death* here refers to a spiritual separation from God.

If our sins have created a humanly insurmountable obstacle, then who can remove sin's barrier and rescue us?

The Rescuer

Christianity is the true account of God's personal rescue of man. What man couldn't do for himself, God did for him. Through the person of Jesus Christ, God has provided the way of escape.

But God demonstrates His own love toward us, in that while we were yet sinners, Christ died for us (Romans 5:8).

He made Him who knew no sin to be sin on our behalf, that we might become the righteousness of God in Him (2 Corinthians 5:21).

Jesus said to him, "I am the way, and the truth, and the life; no one comes to the Father, but through Me" (John 14:6).

And there is salvation in no one else; for there is no other name under heaven that has been given among men, by which we must be saved (Acts 4:12).

As seen earlier, the consequence of sin is death. Sin demands a payment. These verses tell us that Christ became our personal payment for our sin. Jesus Christ is God's only provision for man's sin. He died in our place on the cross to tear down the barrier which separated us from God. And He rose again from the grave after three days to defeat death and offer eternal life to all who will believe in Him.

Jesus Christ, God's son, came to earth to deliver God's message of love and salvation for mankind. Christ said, "I am the door; if anyone enters through Me, he shall be saved" (John 10:9).

Christ has provided each of us a way of escape. But just "knowing" that Christ offers us the route of escape from sin and death is not enough. It is more than just an intellectual acknowledgement of His teaching, life, death, and resurrection.

So what is required? What should your response be?

Your Response

Vera Rodriguez's only possible response to the insurmountable barrier was to cry for help. He realized he couldn't save himself. Likewise, you must come to the conclusion that you are helpless to remove sin's barrier — your cry to God must be one of dependence on God's trustworthiness to save you. He will hear your cry of faith — He will remove the obstruction of sin. But *you* must believe. Christ said,

Truly, truly, I say to you, he who hears My word, and believes Him who sent Me, has eternal life, and does not come into judgment, but has passed out of death into life (John 5:24).

Here Christ promises to remove us from the position of separation from God (death), and place us in a new relationship with God by giving us eternal life. But belief here is more than just a mere intellectual assent; it is a commitment of trust and belief that Christ actually did pay for our sins on the cross to bring us out of death into life (a personal relationship with God).

Your faith does not mean that you are working your way to heaven and a relationship with God. It is not our human efforts or goodness that bring us into a right relationship with God, but our faith in His promise to save us. The Scripture is clear: "For by grace you have been saved through faith; and that not of yourselves, it is the gift of God; not as a result of works, that no one should boast" (Ephesians 2:8,9). And again in John 1:12: "But as many as received Him, to them He gave the right to become children of God, even to those who believe in His name."

Receiving Christ means turning to God from self and sin (repenting) and placing faith in Christ for the forgiveness of your sins.

Perhaps at this point you may be saying, "I know all of that. I've heard it before." But have you ever made your own individual commitment to the person of Jesus Christ?

Just as a marriage begins when two people make a personal commitment, so it is with our relationship with God. No amount of knowledge about your fiancé will make him your mate. It is only when two individuals make that personal pledge of commitment to one another that they become husband and wife.

The following six questions may help you clarify what your need is at this moment:

1. Do you wish to know God in a personal way?
2. Do you understand that you are helpless to establish a right relationship with God yourself?
3. Are you willing to turn from your sin (repent) and turn to Christ to follow Him?
4. Do you see that you *need* Christ's provision for your sin?
5. Are you uncertain of where you would spend eternity if you died at this very moment?
6. Would you like to call God your "Heavenly Father"?

If you answered yes to the questions above, you can truly "be rescued" right now by faith.

One of the ways God has given us to express our faith and trust in Him is prayer. Prayer is simply talking with God, and is a way to place our faith and complete dependence on the fact that what God said is true. Why not express your need of God to save you right now by placing your faith in His Son Jesus Christ?

The following is a suggested prayer (your faith in God's promise is essential):

> Lord Jesus, "help." I need You to save me from my sins. Thank You for dying on the cross for all my sins. I now place my complete faith and dependence upon You to forgive those sins and give me eternal life. Live in me now, and begin to make me into the person You want me to be. Thank You for hearing and answering this prayer.

If you prayed that prayer and placed your faith in Jesus Christ as your Lord and Savior, then we have some free information we would like to send you. Written by Dr. Bill Bright, the president and founder of Campus Crusade for Christ, it explains more fully how you can grow as a Christian. Please write us:

> Dennis and Barbara Rainey
> Campus Crusade for Christ
> P. O. Box 23840
> Little Rock, AR 72221

When you placed your faith in Christ to save you, you received the gift of eternal life. Look at the following promise of Scripture:

> And the witness is this, that God has given us eternal life, and this life is in His Son. He who has the Son has the life, he who does not have the Son of God does not have the life. These things I have written to you who believe in the name of the Son of God, in order that you may know that you have eternal life (1 John 5:11-13).

Look at the verses again. What do you have as a result of believing in Christ?

How *certain* can you be that you have eternal life? Answer: You can *know* you have eternal life on the basis of God's promise. Jesus Christ now lives in you.

One last word: Why not tell your mate today of your decision to trust Christ? In Romans 10:9a, Paul encourages us to "confess with [our] mouth Jesus as Lord." Sharing with another your commitment to Christ will affirm your decision.

Like Vera Rodriguez who was rescued from a grave of physical rubble, we who have placed our trust in Christ have been rescued from the rubble of sin and have truly been "born again." We have experienced Christ's freeing power over sin and selfishness in our lives.

We hope you have too.

I am the light of the world; he who follows Me shall not walk in the darkness, but shall have the light of life."[2]

Notes

Introduction

1. James Dobson, "Dr. Dobson Answers Your Questions," *Focus On the Family* (April 1986), p. 5.

Chapter One

1. Maurice Wagner, *The Sensation of Being Somebody* (Grand Rapids, Mich.: Zondervan Publishing House, 1975), p. 67.
2. Dr. Paul Brand and Philip Yancey, *In His Image* (Grand Rapids, Mich.: Zondervan Publishing House, 1984), pp. 25-29.
3. Denis Waitley, *Seeds of Greatness* (Old Tappan, N.J.: Fleming H. Revell Company, 1983), pp. 41-42.
4. Gloria Steinem, speech at International Women's Year conference, Houston, 1977, as quoted in *To Manipulate a Woman* (pamphlet) (San Diego: Concerned Women for America).
5. Luke 1:37.
6. Josh McDowell, *His Image . . . My Image* (San Bernardino, Calif.: Here's Life Publishers, 1984).

Chapter Two

1. Edwards Park, "A Phantom Division Played a Role in Germany's Defeat," *Smithsonian* (April 1985), p. 138.
2. Dorothy Corkille Briggs, *Your Child's Self-Esteem* (Garden City, N.J.: Doubleday & Company, Inc., 1975), p. 49.
3. H. Norman Wright, *Improving Your Self-Image* (Eugene, Ore.: Harvest House Publishers, 1983), pp. 7-8.
4. Ibid., p. 8.
5. Denis Waitley, *Seeds of Greatness* (Old Tappan, N.J.: Fleming H. Revell Company, 1983), p. 47.

Chapter Three

1. Ovid Demaris, "The Other Side of Laughter," *Parade* (May 5, 1985), pp. 4-9.
2. Dr. W. Hugh Missildine, *Your Inner Child of the Past* (New York: Simon & Schuster, Inc., 1963), p. 87.

Chapter Four

1. Hebrews 4:12.
2. John 8:32.
3. Luke 6:38.
4. Galatians 6:9.
5. Mary Mapes Dodge, *Hans Brinker* (New York: Grosset & Dunlap, Inc., 1984), pp. 154-57.
6. 2 Corinthians 3:18.
7. Galatians 6:7.
8. 2 Corinthians 3:5.
9. 2 Corinthians 12:9,10.

Chapter Five

1. This concept was first taught us by Don and Sally Meredith. Don is the president and founder of Christian Family Life.
2. Genesis 2:24.
3. 1 John 4:18.

Chapter Six

1. Ephesians 4:32.
2. Deuteronomy 5:16.
3. Romans 12:1,2.
4. Philippians 3:13b.
5. 1 Peter 5:8.
6. Ephesians 6:10,11.
7. Revelation 12:10.

Chapter Seven

1. Psalm 33:6,9.
2. © 1981, Fair Hill Music. All rights reserved. Used by permission.
3. Ibid.
4. Ecclesiastes 12:11.
5. Ephesians 4:25.

Chapter Eight

1. Philippians 4:8.
2. See Matthew 7:24-27.
3. Ecclesiastes 3:1,2,4.
4. See James 1:2-8.
5. See John 15:1-17.
6. John 15:2.

Chapter Nine
1. Exodus 3:11.
2. Exodus 3:12.
3. See Exodus 3:13.
4. Exodus 4:10.
5. See Exodus 4:13.
6. John 8:32.
7. Ephesians 4:32.
8. Colossians 3:13.

Chapter Ten
1. "Wishin' and Hopin'," Burt Bacharach and Hal David. Reprinted by permission. Blue Seas Music, Inc., N.Y., © 1969, Jonathan Music Co., Inc. Assigned to Blue Seas Music, Inc., and JAC Music Co.
2. John 14:21.

Chapter Eleven
1. James 1:22-24.
2. Hebrews 11:6.
3. 1 Samuel 2:12.
4. 1 Samuel 2:17.
5. 1 Samuel 2:30b.
6. See Matthew 5:13-16.
7. James 5:16b.
8. James 4:2b.
9. 1 Thessalonians 5:17.
10. C. S. Lewis, *Beyond Personality,* reprinted in *Mere Christianity* (New York: MacMillan Publishing Co., 1952), p. 189-90.

Chapter Twelve
1. Proverbs 27:17.

Chapter Thirteen
1. Dennis Rainey, *My Soapbox,* newsletter published by Family Ministry (January 1985).
2. See Genesis 1:26.
3. Ephesians 5:15-17.

Chapter Fourteen
1. Charles Colson, "Standing Tough Against All Odds," *Christianity Today* (Sept. 6, 1985), pp. 25-33.
2. Ibid.

3. See Genesis 22:17.
4. See Psalm 147:4.
5. See Matthew 10:29,30.
6. Psalm 106:25.
7. Elizabeth D. Dodds, *Marriage to a Difficult Man,* as quoted in *Where Have All the Mothers Gone?* by Brenda Hunter, (Grand Rapids, Mich: Zondervan Publishing House, 1982), p. 109.
8. See 2 Timothy 2:2.

Chapter Fifteen

1. Adapted from Tom Peters, *The Excellence Challenge* tape series, (Waltham, Mass.: EXCEL/MEDIA, INC., 1984).
2. 1 Peter 3:7b.
3. 1 Peter 3:7a.
4. 1 Peter 3:7b.
5. 1 Samuel 22:2.
6. 1 Chronicles 12:21.

Chapter Sixteen

1. Adapted from Joyce Brothers, *What Every Woman Should Know About Men* (New York: Ballantine Books, 1981), pp. 29-34.
2. Jill Renich, *To Have and to Hold* (Grand Rapids, Mich.: Zondervan Publishing House, 1972), p. 55.
3. Brothers, *What Every Woman,* p. 147.
4. Renich, *To Have,* p. 55.
5. Brothers, *What Every Woman,* p. 154.

Chapter Seventeen

1. Hebrews 12:1-3.
2. 2 Corinthians 3:18.
3. See Matthew 5:13-16.

Appendix

1. "El Temblor! Tragedy in Mexico City," (UPI), *Reader's Digest* (January 1986), pp. 63-64.
2. John 8:12.

From One of America's Top Homebuilders

If you've grown as a result of this book, we encourage you to strengthen your marriage further by attending a "weekend to remember" at one of our Family Life Conferences. Dennis and Barbara speak at several conferences each year and the material in this book is an outgrowth of more than ten years of their ministry to families around the U.S. through the Family Ministry. If you would like to receive information on an upcoming conference in your area, please complete the coupon below.

The Family Ministry also has provided *The Homebuilder Series* as a small group Bible study designed to provide positive solutions based on biblical, workable principles. It will strengthen your marriage, pull your family closer together, and give you practical "how to's" on building a distinctly Christian marriage. Check below to receive information on this study.

Dennis publishes a monthly newsletter, *My Soapbox,* which covers a variety of topics on the home, the family and the Christian life. If you would like to hear from us on a regular basis, we would be happy to send you a free subscription. Please check below.
Please return the coupon to: FAMILY MINISTRY
P.O. Box 23840
Little Rock, AR 72221

TELL ME MORE!
I am interested in the following (please check)
_____ Family Life Conference brochure
_____ Homebuilder Series
_____ *My Soapbox* (Dennis's monthly newsletter)
Name _____
Address _____
City _____ State _____ Zip _____
